BLUE-COLLAR LEADERSHIP® TOOLBOX TIPS

60 Micro-Lessons to Maximize Your Influence

Volume 1

Mack Story

Copyright © 2021 Mack Story

All rights reserved.

ISBN-13: 9798511255781

DEDICATION

To those who have a strong desire to intentionally climb to the next level and beyond. Keep climbing!

CONTENTS

Introduction

Tip #1: Give Credit	2
Tip #2: Believe in Others	4
Tip #3: Grow on Purpose	6
Tip #4: Uncommon Sense	8
Tip #5: The "I" in Team	10
Tip #6: Be Better Tomorrow	12
Tip #7: The Secret to Success	14
Tip #8: Someone is Always Watching	16
Tip #9: Potential is Unlimited	18
Tip #10: Focus on the Mirror	20
Tip #11: Response Matters Most	22
Tip #12: Choose Your Future	24
Tip #13: Courage is Contagious	26
Tip #14: Like Attracts Like	28
Tip #15: Character Counts	30

Tip #16: Success on the Inside	32
Tip #17: Leaders have Followers	34
Tip #18: Positions are Overrated	36
Tip #19: Great Leaders were Great Followers	38
Tip #20: Learn to Listen	40
Tip #21: Don't Stumble, Be Humble	42
Tip #22: Ask for Responsibility	44
Tip #23: Help Others Succeed	46
Tip #24: Be the First to Help	48
Tip #25: Overdeliver	50
Tip #26: Sooner than Expected	52
Tip #27: Better than Expected	54
Tip #28: Stretch Intentionally	56
Tip #29: Develop Intentionally	58
Tip #30: Bet on Yourself	60
Tip #31: Be Growth-Oriented	64
Tip #32: Be Trustworthy	66
Tip #33: Be Humble	68

Tip #34: Be Responsible	70
Tip #35: Be Positive	72
Tip #36: Be Flexible	74
Tip #37: Be Focused	76
Tip #38: Be Disciplined	78
Tip #39: Be Intentional	80
Tip #40: Be Driven	82
Tip #41: Be Inspired	84
Tip #42: Be Proud	86
Tip #43: Be Brave	88
Tip #44: Be Teachable	90
Tip #45: Be Open-Minded	92
Tip #46: Be Approachable	94
Tip #47: Be Helpful	96
Tip #48: Be Observant	98
Tip #49: Be Engaged	100
Tip #50: Be Present	102
Tip #51: Be Understanding	104

Tip #52: Be Competent	106
Tip #53: Be Certain	108
Tip #54: Be Motivational	110
Tip #55: Be Inspirational	112
Tip #56: Be Aware	114
Tip #57: Be Careful	116
Tip #58: Be Optimistic	118
Tip #59: Be Realistic	120
Tip #60: Be Relentless	122

INTRODUCTION

Blue-Collar Leadership® Toolbox Tips is filled with 60 micro-lessons intended to provoke thought and raise awareness.

These micro-lessons can be studied alone or introduced in a team or group setting to initiate growth and facilitate discussion. Each micro-lesson can be read in 1-2 minutes. However, additional group discussion is encouraged.

Each micro-lesson begins with a principle that, if applied, will help you increase your influence. Life is always better with more influence, not less.

As you read each micro-lesson, look for ways to validate and reinforce what you're learning. Do this by reflecting on times when you or others got it right and gained influence or times when you or others got it wrong and lost influence.

Section 1 is based on Mack's book, *Blue-Collar Leadership®: Leading from the Front Lines*, which is focused on helping you become a high impact individual.

Section 2 is based on Mack's book, *Blue-Collar Leadership® & Teamwork: 30 Traits of High Impact Players,* which is focused on helping you become a high impact team player.

High impact people are always more valuable, more effective, and more influential. High performance teams are filled with high impact people. Be more.

SECTION 1

TOOLBOX TIPS BASED ON "BLUE-COLLAR LEADERSHIP®: LEADING FROM THE FRONT LINES"

🔧 Toolbox Tip #1

Who we are matters. We should give credit to others when things go right and take responsibility when things go wrong.

Why It Matters: We build trust and increase our influence with others when we have the personal integrity to take responsibility when things go wrong and the security to give credit when things go right.

What We Do: We look for opportunities to intentionally give others credit when things go right. We look for opportunities to take responsibility when things go wrong by asking, *"How could I have prevented this from happening?"*

What We Don't Do: We don't seek credit when things go right. We don't look for others to blame when things go wrong.

Bad Example(s): We give credit to others publicly but seek credit for ourselves privately. We take the blame publicly but blame others privately.

> **Think About This**
>
> "No amount of personal competency can compensate for personal insecurity."
> ~ Wayne Smith

Ask Yourself: What would cause me to take credit when things go right? What would cause me to blame others when things go wrong?

What Do You Think?

🔧 Toolbox Tip #2

When we believe in someone unconditionally, we believe in them because they have the potential to be more and do more.

Why It Matters: We strengthen relationships and increase our influence when we unconditionally believe in the abilities of others. When we express belief in others, they are more likely to make an effort to live up to our expectations.

What We Do: We look for opportunities to encourage others when they doubt themselves or their abilities.

What We Don't Do: We don't make fun of those attempting new things. We don't give others a reason to doubt themselves.

Bad Example(s): We express our belief in others publicly but question them and their abilities privately.

Think About This

"The dictionary defines belief as trust, faith, and confidence. However, that definition is selfish and requires judgment. I think we need to change the way we believe in people. We need to redefine the way we believe in people. We should redefine belief as encouragement, empowerment, and engagement. This definition is selfless and doesn't require judgment." ~ Joshua Encarnacion

Ask Yourself: When has someone believed in me when I didn't believe in myself? How did it make me feel? What's stopping me from being that person for someone else? Who could benefit from my belief in them?

What Do You Think?

🔧 Toolbox Tip #3

Growth doesn't just happen. We must become intentional and make it happen.

Why It Matters: This Toolbox Tip increases our influence because we are communicating our desire to be more, learn more, give more, and to accomplish more. We are communicating we are not satisfied and no longer willing to remain average.

What We Do: We must focus on developing our weaknesses relative to our character (who we are) because these weaknesses will hold us back like an anchor. We must focus on developing our strengths relative to our competency (what we know: talent, abilities, skills, knowledge) because these strengths will launch us like a rocket.

What We Don't Do: We don't wait for others to develop us. We don't do only what is required by others. We don't turn down opportunities for growth and development. We don't make excuses for not growing.

Bad Example(s): We appear on board about growth publicly while we privately talk bad about the process and those who are challenging us to grow.

> ### Think About This
>
> "You don't have to be sick to get better."
> ~ Michael Josephson

Ask Yourself: Am I only doing what is required? What would change if I always did more than required? How would I benefit? How can I get started? What's stopping me?

What Do You Think?

🔧 Toolbox Tip #4

Common sense is never enough. What is common sense isn't always common practice. Often, to do what is commonly understood, we must have uncommon sense.

Why It Matters: Uncommon sense increases our influence because doing what we and others know we should do demonstrates that we have self-discipline and can lead ourselves well.

What We Do: We set the example for others to follow. We actually start doing what we know we should be doing. We do the right thing, at the right time, for the right reason.

What We Don't Do: We don't believe others should behave a certain way without behaving that way ourselves. We don't believe others need to develop their character without developing our own.

Bad Example(s): We say we believe in something in front of others, but we beat around the bush and make excuses for why we haven't embraced it ourselves. Remember, our development is personal, but it's not private.

Think About This

"There's a fundamental difference between being in an organization where people are trusted and given the latitude to use their judgment, and one where people are seen merely as cogs in some machine, neither trusted nor respected for their common sense." ~ Kouzes & Posner

Ask Yourself: What do I do that wastes my time, energy, and money? Why do I do these things? What things can I start doing that will help me climb to the next level and beyond? Why am I not doing these things already? How can I start?

What Do You Think?

🔧 Toolbox Tip #5

There is an "I" in team. Every team is made up of "I"ndividuals. Every person on a team is an "I" and has the potential to lead (influence) the team, positively or negatively. *Note: You can read the related chapter on page 147.*

Why It Matters: Our influence is not about us, but it starts with us. Choosing to become a high impact team player communicates we understand we are part of something bigger than ourselves. When we value our team, we build trust with our team.

What We Do: First, we lead ourselves well, so we are seen as a positive role model. Then, we intentionally look for ways to develop positive influence by helping our team members succeed.

What We Don't Do: We don't transfer our responsibilities. We don't expect the team to carry our load. We don't wait to be asked or told what to do when we already know what should be done.

Bad Example(s): We publicly offer support to our team and our leader, but we privately do and say things that undermine our team members and our leader.

> **Think About This**
>
> "The most valuable player is the one that makes the most players valuable."
> ~ Peyton Manning

Ask Yourself: Beyond what is required of me, how do I add value to my team? If asked, would others say I am a positive or negative influence? How can I become a more valuable team member?

What Do You Think?

🔧 Toolbox Tip #6

Be better tomorrow. When we become more valuable, we will become more successful. When we make ourselves more valuable, others will make us more successful.

Why It Matters: When we choose to do the things that make us more valuable to the organization, more people in the organization will value us. Becoming more valuable increases our influence. A desire to be successful may or may not increase our influence.

What We Do: We intentionally help and serve others in a way that causes them to realize our value to them or to the team. We help others become successful.

What We Don't Do: We don't let our ego and hunger for success diminish our value and create distrust with others.

Bad Example(s): Publicly we want to be seen as someone who motivates others to accomplish the mission for all the right reasons, but privately we want to manipulate others for all the wrong reasons.

> **Think About This**
>
> "It is the capacity to develop and improve themselves that distinguishes leaders from followers." ~ Bennis & Nanus

Ask Yourself: What will change if I truly become more valuable? To my team? To my leader? To my organization? To my family? What can I do to intentionally get better every day?

What Do You Think?

🔧 Toolbox Tip #7

The secret to our success is knowing we get paid by others, but we are working for ourselves.

Why It Matters. Word of mouth is the most powerful type of advertisement. The person paying us is always our #1 customer and those talking good or bad about us (advertising who we are and how we do what we do) are lifting us up or tearing us down.

What We Do: We do everything we can to generate positive word of mouth about ourselves. When people say positive things, our influence and value increases.

What We Don't Do: We don't do or say things that will lead to negative word of mouth. When people say negative things, our influence and value decreases.

Bad Example(s): When we think others are watching, we behave one way. When we think no one is watching, we behave another way.

> ### Think About This
>
> "Who we are sometimes matters all the time."
> ~ Mack Story

Ask Yourself: What would I do differently if I truly believe I am working for myself? What would others see when they looked at me? How would I interact with others?

What Do You Think?

🔧 *Toolbox Tip #8*

Someone is always watching us. We are always teaching what we're modeling, regardless of what we're teaching.

Why It Matters: Modeling what we are teaching reveals high integrity to those who are watching and listening. High integrity increases our influence while low integrity decreases our influence.

What We Do: We think before we speak. We align our actions with our words.

What We Don't Do: We don't say one thing and do another. We don't expect others to behave in ways that we don't.

Bad Example(s): When we teach others to lead themselves in a way that we aren't willing to lead ourselves, we are teaching one thing while modeling another.

Think About This

"Nothing is more confusing than people who give good advice, but set a bad example."
~ Norman Vincent Peale

"Nothing is more convincing than people who give good advice and set a good example."
~ John C. Maxwell

Ask Yourself: Do my actions always match my words? At work? At home?

What Do You Think?

🔧 *Toolbox Tip #9*

Our potential is unlimited. We should always be grateful, but never satisfied.

Why It Matters: Applying this Toolbox Tip increases our influence by communicating to others that we appreciate and value being where we are while having a desire to be more and do more. This reveals we are growth-oriented. Growing organizations value growing people.

What We Do: We express gratitude for what we have and what we do. We communicate our desire to grow and learn by trying new things and seeking new knowledge.

What We Don't Do: We don't moan and groan about where we are or what we're doing. We don't settle for remaining the same. We don't wait for others to develop us.

Bad Example(s): When we complain about our current circumstances, resist change, and blame others for our lack of opportunities, we are limiting ourselves and reducing our influence.

> ### Think About This
>
> "Nothing is given to man on earth except a potential and the material on which to actualize it. The potential is a superlative machine: his consciousness; but it is a machine without a spark plug, a machine of which his own will has to be the spark plug, the self-starter and the driver; he has to discover how to use it and he has to keep it in constant action. The material is the whole of the universe, with no limits set to the knowledge he can acquire and to the enjoyment of life he can achieve. But everything he needs or desires has to be learned, discovered and produced by him—by his own choice, by his own effort, by his own mind."
> ~ Ayn Rand

Ask Yourself: Would those who know me well say I am grateful? How often do I express gratitude to my family? My boss? Would those who know me well say I have a hunger for professional growth? For personal growth?

What Do You Think?

ary # 🔧 Toolbox Tip #10

We should focus on the mirror. The face we see least is our own. We don't know what we need to know about ourselves.

Why It Matters: The solution to nearly every problem we will ever face can be found simply by looking in the mirror. Different people will experience the same problem differently because of who they are on the inside, not because of what's happening on the outside.

What We Do: We change what needs to change instead of what is easy to change. We take responsibility for ourselves and our circumstances. When we take responsibility, our influence increases.

What We Don't Do: We don't transfer responsibility. We don't blame others for our problems or our circumstances. When we blame others, our influence decreases.

Bad Example(s): When things go wrong or we're not happy with our circumstances, instead of looking in the mirror at ourselves as the cause, we look out the window for someone to blame.

> ### Think About This
>
> "Self-mastery is the hardest job you will ever tackle. If you do not conquer self, you will be conquered by self. You may see at the same time both your best friend and your worst enemy, by simply stepping in front
> of the mirror." ~ Napoleon Hill

Ask Yourself: How am I responsible for my problems? How am I responsible for my circumstances? What can I do to improve my situation? How can take action?

What Do You Think?

🔧 Toolbox Tip #11

What happens to us in important, but our response to what happens to us is most important.

Why It Matters. When something happens, we have the power to pause and choose our response. When we respond positively and proactively, we increase our influence. When we respond negatively and reactively, we decrease our influence.

What We Do: We intentionally pause and consider how our response will impact our influence and how it will impact our future. Then, we choose a response that offers the greatest benefit.

What We Don't Do: We don't choose our response based on our emotions and feelings. We don't respond before we have determined a response that will make the situation better, not worse.

Bad Example(s): Something happens and we become reactive, sad, mad, or frustrated. We forget to pause and simply react immediately. When we do this, we are likely to respond in anger which decreases our influence, damages relationships, and worsens our circumstances.

> ### *Think About This*
>
> "The same thing can happen to two different people, yet they respond in two completely different ways. One positive. One negative. What's the difference? Their values and the story they tell themselves about what happened, how it will affect them, and what they should do about it." ~ Mack Story

Ask Yourself: Are my responses naturally reactive (negative) or proactive (positive)? How will better responses benefit me? How has my past responses impacted my influence?

What Do You Think?

🔧 Toolbox Tip #12

Our future is in us now. If we don't choose our future, someone else will.

Why It Matters: Our future is defined and refined by the choices we do or don't make every day. When we avoid making a choice, we have made a choice to be acted upon. When we make good choices, our life gets better. When we make bad choices, our life gets worse.

What We Do: We determine who we are and where we are. We determine who we want to become and where we want to go which reveals our success gap. To close the gap, before making a choice we ask ourselves, *"Will what I'm about to do move me in the right direction?"* If the answer is yes and we do it, the gap narrows. If the answer is no and we do it, the gap widens.

What We Don't Do: We don't make choices without considering the impact on our future. We don't allow others to determine our future. We don't make choices that will widen our success gap.

Bad Example(s): Doing only what is required of us which means we are allowing others to plan and shape our future. What do they likely have planned for us? Most often, it's not much.

> ### Think About This
>
> "We are anxious to improve our circumstances but unwilling to improve ourselves.
> We therefore remain bound." ~ James Allen

Ask Yourself: What future do I want to create? Am I taking intentional steps to turn my vision into my reality? What's stopping me?

What Do You Think?

🔧 Toolbox Tip #13

Courage is contagious. Courage allows average people to achieve exceptional results.

Why It Matters: This Toolbox Tip increases our influence because it takes courage to do the right things at the right time for the right reasons while those around us are trying to get us to do the wrong things for the wrong reasons.

What We Do: We seek the truth when it's hard or unpopular. We change what needs to be changed, not what is easy to change. We model the values we believe in even when others do not. We learn and grow knowing it will expose our weaknesses. We choose to be proactive when we feel like being reactive.

What We Don't Do: We don't give in when the going gets tough. We don't compromise on our values when others pressure us to do so. We don't stay in toxic relationships. We don't accept influence from those not aligned with our values and mission.

Bad Example(s): Demonstrating courage for the wrong reasons. When we use our influence to lead others down the wrong path, they end up making decisions that will negatively impact their lives, personally and professionally. Having the courage to negatively influence others is a weakness, not a strength.

> ### Think About This
>
> "While one person hesitates because he feels inferior, another person is making mistakes and becoming superior." ~ Henry C. Link

Ask Yourself: What would change if I had more courage? Where in my life is a lack of courage holding me back? Do I truly have the courage to stand alone when necessary? What does my behavior reveal?

What Do You Think?

🔧 Toolbox Tip #14

We attract those who are like us. Those who like us the most are also the most like us.

Why It Matters: We become the average of the five people we voluntarily hang around the most. It's true. We start talking like they talk, acting like they act, dressing like they dress, eating what they eat, drinking what they drink, doing what they do, and most importantly, we begin to think like they think and believe what they believe. We are likely to also get the results they get.

What We Do: We intentionally develop our character in an effort to attract others with higher level character. We end relationships with people who are not living like we want to be living. We have the courage to stand alone until we are capable of attracting people with better character into our life.

What We Don't Do: We don't associate with people who are not positively influencing us. We don't allow others to decide where we are going. We don't lower our standards to remain friends with those who aren't going where we're going.

Bad Example(s): Choosing to stay in bad relationships, personally and/or professionally, for any reason. If we are choosing to let others negatively impact our lives, it's our fault, not their fault.

> **Think About This**
>
> "One of the most expensive things you could ever do is pay attention to the wrong people."
> ~ Henry Cloud

Ask Yourself: What is the true character of the five people I voluntarily associate with? How am I being influenced by them? Positively? Negatively? Where are they truly headed? Forward? Backward? Are they stuck? Am I stuck?

What Do You Think?

🔧 Toolbox Tip #15

Character counts. Who we are on the inside determines what others see, feel, and experience on the outside.

Why It Matters: When it comes to character, it's not about what we know. It's about who we are. People are most often hired for what they know, but they are most often fired for who they are. Our character will either launch us or limit us. Character is personal, but it's not private.

What We Do: We intentionally make choices that reveal a high degree of character. We make and keep commitments. We do what we said we would do, when we said we would do it, how we said we would do it, because we said we would do it. We ensure our motive, agenda, and behavior are aligned with positive, character-based principles. We say and do things that build trust.

What We Don't Do: We don't lie. We don't make and break commitments. We don't talk about others behind their backs. We don't fail to stand for what's right. We don't hang around negative people. We don't do or say things that create distrust.

Bad Example(s): Blaming others for our behavior when things don't go our way. Speaking to others in anger. Pretending to know when we don't know. Allowing our pride and ego to prevent us from doing the right thing.

> ### Think About This
>
> "Our reputations do not come from how we talk about ourselves. Our reputations come from how others talk about us." ~ Simon Sinek

Ask Yourself: Do I ever blame others for my behavior? Do others control me, or do I control me? Who is responsible for my behavior? What does my behavior communicate to others?

What Do You Think?

🔧 Toolbox Tip #16

We have far more than we need to succeed on the outside because it's provided for us. The question is, do we have what we need to succeed on the inside?

Why It Matters: We can't climb to the top of the mountain with base camp character. Our character will either maximize or minimize our success.

What We Do: We intentionally develop our character to maximize our influence and leverage our competency (talents, abilities, skills, & knowledge).

What We Don't Do: We don't say and do things that will minimize our influence with other people, especially those of high character. We don't expect what we have not earned.

Bad Example(s): Remaining a part of the problem by looking outward and casting blame at others when things aren't going our way instead of looking inward and becoming a part of the solution to ensure things do go our way.

Think About This

"A sign of wisdom and maturity is when you come to terms with the realization that your decisions cause your rewards and consequences. You are responsible for your life, and your ultimate success depends on the choices you make." ~ Denis Waitley

Ask Yourself: How do I deal with things that don't go my way? Do I embrace change or resist change? What choices do I need to make to become more valuable?

What Do You Think?

🔧 Toolbox Tip #17

Leaders have followers who want to follow them. Bosses have workers who have to follow them. The difference between a leader and a boss is their values.

Why It Matters: Leadership is influence. We all have influence, at work and at home. Therefore, we are all leaders.

What We Do: We value authentic, character-based influence based on a foundation of motivation and inspiration. We respect everyone at every level. We value building meaningful relationships that increase our influence. We look in the mirror and work to improve our leadership ability daily.

What We Don't Do: We don't value or seek authority or control over others. We don't seek a position of authority, so others will *"have to"* follow us. We don't disrespect others. We don't think we are better than others.

Bad Example(s): Low impact leaders make people feel used, dumb, powerless, guilty, small, alone, weak, defeated, and tired. Instead of serving their team, they believe their team is there to serve them.

> ### Think About This
>
> "A leader is someone who has followers. If there are no followers, there is no leader. A person may have subordinates, workers, admirers, associates, co-workers, friends, and people who report to him or her, a person may have authority over other people, a person may hold an elective office, and a person may influence a large number of people, but that does not make that person a leader if there are no followers. A follower is someone that has chosen a leader." ~
> Jimmy Collins

Ask Yourself: Do I like having authority? What does my answer reveal about me? Is it hard for me to get those who don't report to me to follow me? What does this reveal about my influence?

What Do You Think?

🔧 *Toolbox Tip #18*

Leadership positions are overrated. If we can't lead without a leadership position, we won't lead with one.

Why It Matters: We will always have more options and greater success when we learn to lead without a leadership position. High impact leaders don't need a position of authority to make things happen. They just need a team. Our value is multiplied when we can lead without a position.

What We Do: We learn to lead up, down, left, and right without a leadership position. We learn to influence people because of who we are and what we know. We make things happen!

What We Don't Do: We don't wait to be given a leadership position before we choose to learn how to lead. We don't rest upon our position, authority, or the lack of it. We don't make excuses.

Bad Example(s): Waiting to be given a leadership position before beginning to read and study about leadership. Leaders who think they don't need to learn because they already have a leadership position. Those without a leadership position thinking they can't lead because no one reports to them.

> ### Think About This
>
> "Saying '*a position makes someone a leader*' is like saying '*giving someone a whistle makes them a coach.*'" ~ Gary Arblaster

Ask Yourself: What character traits do I have that increase my influence with others? What character traits do I have that decrease my influence with others? What do I need to change?

What Do You Think?

🔧 *Toolbox Tip #19*

Followers choose leaders. All great leaders were first great followers.

Why It Matters: We are all following (being influenced by others), and we are all leading (influencing others). Our ability to follow others well is an indicator of our ability to lead others well. If we don't follow well, we won't lead well. When high impact leaders are looking for others to develop and promote, they seek out high impact followers.

What We Do: We follow well by supporting our leaders and our team members. We intentionally grow and develop ourselves in an effort to be better followers and better leaders. When we do, we make our leaders better and our team better.

What We Don't Do: We don't follow blindly as if we can't think for ourselves. We don't do only what's required. We don't wait for others to solve our problems. We don't avoid responsibility.

Bad Example(s): Pointing out problems to leaders before thinking about and identifying a solution. Believing our development is the responsibility of our leaders.

> ### Think About This
>
> "An inexperienced worker may not realize that a leader will leave a follower a lot of opportunities to express himself. A worker will shirk the responsibility and wait for instructions. A follower, on the other hand, will grab the opportunity and run with it." ~ Jimmy Collins

Ask Yourself: How well do I follow? What can I do to improve? How well do I lead? What can I do to improve?

What Do You Think?

🔧 *Toolbox Tip #20*

We learn when we're listening, not when we're speaking. Seek first to understand, then to be understood.

Why It Matters: One of the best ways to grow our influence with others is to first allow them to influence us. We do this by listening with the intent to understand, not reply.

What We Do: We let others go first. We express a desire to first understand the other's point of view. We acknowledge the feelings and emotions behind their words.

What We Don't Do: We don't dominate the conversation. We don't say what we have to say quickly without a desire to understand the other's perspective. We don't listen without listening.

Bad Example(s): Attempting to get others to understand us before we have demonstrated that we completely and fully understand them.

> ### Think About This
>
> "You can win more friends with your ears than with your mouth. People who feel like they're being listened to feel accepted and appreciated. They feel like they're being taken seriously and what they say really matters."
> ~ Harvey Mackay

Ask Yourself: How well do I listen? What can I do to become a better listener? What relationships will improve if I choose to listen better?

What Do You Think?

🔧 Toolbox Tip #21

We should think of ourselves less. There's a fine line between arrogance and confidence. It's called humility. Be humble, so you don't stumble.

Why It Matters: Humility is a character trait that reveals strength, not weakness. Our level of humility reveals our level of security. Secure people are humble. Humble people want to serve others. Insecure people are prideful and ego driven. Prideful people want to be served by others.

What We Do: We have a *"we"* attitude. We look for ways to help and serve our leaders and our team members. We let others go before we do. We make success about the team. We give credit.

What We Don't Do: We don't have a *"me first"* attitude. We don't expect our leaders or our team members to serve us. We don't always have to be first. We don't make it about us. We don't want credit.

Bad Example(s): Taking credit for someone else's idea. Taking credit for someone else's work. Placing our own needs above the needs of our team. Acting like we have all the answers or the only answers.

> ### Think About This
>
> "People with humility don't think less of themselves.
> They just think about
> themselves less." ~ Ken Blanchard

Ask Yourself: Would I rather follow an arrogant person or a confident person? Which would have more authentic influence? What do my leader and my team members see and feel when they're around me? Am I arrogant? Am I confident? Am I both at different times?

What Do You Think?

🔧 Toolbox Tip #22

If we want to climb to the next level and beyond, we should take more responsibility. The quickest way to increase our influence is to get results.

Why It Matters: When we accept more responsibility, we will gain more influence with those who are responsible for moving the organization forward.

What We Do: We share our ideas openly and ask to implement them. We look for opportunities to accept and take more responsibility. We gain experience from the additional responsibility. We become more valuable because of the experience.

What We Don't Do: We don't avoid responsibility. We don't look for ways to do less. We don't keep quiet when we have an idea because we're afraid we'll be asked to implement it. We don't say, *"I'm just here to get a check."* or *"I'm just here to do my eight and hit the gate."*

Bad Example(s): Standing on the sidelines when things go wrong. Blaming others for not providing information we could have asked for. Blaming others for doing what we should have prevented them from doing. Letting others *"learn the hard way"* when we could have shown them an easier or better way.

> **Think About This**
>
> "Total responsibility for failure is a difficult thing to accept, and taking ownership when things go wrong requires extraordinary humility and courage."
> ~ Jocko Willink, U.S. Navy Seal Commander

Ask Yourself: What can I do to accept more responsibility at work? At home? How and where will my influence increase when I do?

What Do You Think?

🔧 Toolbox Tip #23

Helping others succeed ensures our success.

Why It Matters: Success is about me. Significance is about we. The most valuable people are not only successful. They are also significant because they have helped others become successful.

What We Do: We share knowledge. We help others stand out and get noticed for their contributions, knowledge, skills, and abilities. We teach others to do what we do. We have an abundance mindset and know there is plenty of everything for everyone.

What We Don't Do: We don't hoard knowledge or resources. We don't hold team members back. We don't have a scarcity mindset believing there is only so much of everything, so we must get our share before someone else gets it.

Bad Example(s): Using others to get ahead without regard for their success. Attempting to make others look bad, so we can look good. Withholding information that could help others in order to make ourselves look more knowledgeable and more informed.

> ### Think About This
>
> "If you want to increase your results, expect to win—not only for yourself, but also for your team. Not at all costs, but honorably. Not at the expense of others, but in conjunction with others. Expecting to win—and expecting others to win—is a fundamental approach of helping to bring it about."
> ~ Stephen M. R. Covey

Ask Yourself: What happens to someone's influence when they hoard knowledge? Am I more likely to share knowledge or hoard knowledge? How will my answer impact my influence? Will hoarding knowledge cause others to speak positively or negatively about me?

What Do You Think?

🔧 Toolbox Tip #24

We should be the first to help. When we help first, we always maximize our influence, not only with everyone we are helping, but also with everyone who is watching.

Why It Matters: Everyone remembers the first to help; few remember the second.

What We Do: Look for opportunities to help others. Act immediately. Help others in small ways because with people the little things are the big things.

What We Don't Do: Don't avoid helping others. Don't expect something in return. Don't wait to see if someone else will help.

Bad Example(s): Waiting and hoping someone else will help first, so you don't have to. Helping publicly and complaining about it privately. Denying someone's need for assistance because *"It's not my job."*

> ### *Think About This*
>
> "Helping others when they least expect it makes you stand out from the crowd.
> Look for ways to stand out." ~ Mack Story

Ask Yourself: When I see someone who needs help, how often am I the first to help? When I need help, do I notice who helped me first? How do I feel about them? Does their influence increase or decrease?

What Do You Think?

🔧 Toolbox Tip #25

As Wayne Dyer stated, *"It's never crowded along the extra mile."* We should overdeliver by doing more than expected.

Why It Matters: Doing more than expected increases our influence. Doing less than expected decreases our influence. If we are willing to do more than we are paid to do, eventually we will be paid for doing more.

What We Do: We intentionally look for ways to go above and beyond. We do more with a good attitude. We do more because we want to not because we have to. We strive to be exceptional.

What We Don't Do: We don't do only what we have to do. We don't do less than expected. We don't wait to be told to do more.

Bad Example(s): Having to be told to do more when it's obvious that we could have and should have done more. Having others finish what we started. Doing less than expected. Moaning and groaning about what we do.

> **Think About This**
>
> "Never mistake efforts and intentions for results." ~ Dick Vermeil

Ask Yourself: When someone does more than I expect, does their influence increase with me? Why? Where, when, and how can I do more than expected?

What Do You Think?

🔧 Toolbox Tip #26

We should do things sooner than expected.

Why It Matters: Doing things sooner than expected increases our influence. Doing things later than expected decreases our influence. It's been said, *"The wise do at once what the fool does at last."*

What We Do: We intentionally look for opportunities to finish early. We have the discipline to finish early even if it means we'll be given more to do because doing more than expected also increases our influence.

What We Don't Do: We don't finish late. We don't take longer than promised. We don't make promises or commitments we can't keep.

Bad Example(s): Waiting until the last minute to complete an assignment or project. Committing to finishing on time, but being late. Making excuses on the backend to cover our lack of commitment on the frontend.

> ### Think About This
>
> "Success is not the result of making money. Earning money is the result of success — and success is in direct proportion to our service."
> ~ Earl Nightingale

Ask Yourself: How do I feel when someone does something sooner than I expect? As a result, do they have more or less influence? Where, when, and how can I do things sooner than expected?

What Do You Think?

🔧 *Toolbox Tip #27*

We should do things better than expected.

Why It Matters: Doing things better than expected increases our influence. Doing things worse than expected decreases our influence. When we pay more attention to the details and exceed expectations, people pay more attention to us. Shiny objects get noticed…so do shiny people.

What We Do: We look for ways to do a better job than expected. We look for ways to improve the process by increasing production, reducing costs, and improving safety and quality. We intentionally look for ways to get better without being asked or required.

What We Don't Do: We don't do things worse than expected. We don't do things only as expected. We don't measure ourselves against others expectations but rather against our abilities.

Bad Example(s): Always meeting expectations. Never exceeding expectations. Doing only what you are paid to do even when you have the time and ability to do it better.

> ### Think About This
>
> "It is the practice of the majority of people to perform no more service than they feel they are being paid to perform. Fully 80% of all whom I have analyzed were suffering on account of this great mistake. You need have no fear of competition from the person who says, *I'm not paid to do that, therefore I'll not do it.*' They will never be a dangerous competitor for your job." ~ Napoleon Hill

Ask Yourself: Who has more influence with me, someone who does things better than expected or worse than expected? Why? Do I consistently do things better than expected?

What Do You Think?

🔧 Toolbox Tip #28

We should stretch ourselves intentionally because all of our growth happens beyond our comfort zone.

Why It Matters. Others will only stretch us when doing so will help them accomplish their mission. Most often however, we must stretch ourselves in order to accomplish our mission.

What We Do: We support change. We embrace change. We initiate change. We lead change. We embrace challenge. We seek challenges. We seek new opportunities.

What We Don't Do: We don't wait for others to stretch us. We don't resist change. We don't turn down opportunities because we're afraid or uncomfortable.

Bad Example(s): Remaining the same in a changing world. Only learning and doing what is required to do the job. Waiting for others to challenge us, grow us, and develop us. Working hard on our jobs, but not working at all on ourselves.

> ### *Think About This*
>
> "If you work hard on your job, you can make a living. But, if you work hard on yourself, you can make a fortune." ~ Jim Rohn

Ask Yourself: What am I currently doing, beyond what is required, to stretch myself to the next level and beyond? If I don't do it, who will? What would change if I climb to the next level? What's stopping me?

What Do You Think?

🔧 Toolbox Tip #29

We should develop ourselves intentionally and consistently. If we won't invest in developing ourselves, why should anyone else?

Why It Matters: Developing ourselves increases our influence. If we don't develop ourselves, we should be prepared to be left behind by those who do.

What We Do: We raise our own bar by focusing on educational, motivational, and inspirational content. In the area of personal growth and development, we read books, listen to audio books, or watch videos. We volunteer for new jobs and new training to gain new experience.

What We Don't Do: We don't wait for others to grow and develop us. We don't remain the same in a changing world. We don't rest on what we accomplished in the past to take us to where we want to be in the future.

Bad Example(s): Making excuses when we can't get ahead. Making excuses when others pass us by. Blaming others for our circumstances, lack of opportunity, or lack of growth. Wasting time away from work that could be invested in developing and preparing ourselves for the future.

> ### *Think About This*
>
> "Accidental growth versus intentional growth is about as effective as accidental exercise compared to intentional exercise...not even close. And the results...not even close."
> ~ Mack Story

Ask Yourself: Where am I? Who am I? Where do I want to be? Who do I want to become? How do I close the gap between where I am and where I want to be? What's stopping me?

What Do You Think?

🔧 *Toolbox Tip #30*

We must bet on ourselves. If we won't bet on ourselves, why should anyone else?

Why It Matters: People who believe in themselves have more influence than those who don't. A better tomorrow won't just happen. We must be intentional and make it happen. Living intentionally leads to amazing results. Living accidentally leads to depressing disappointments.

What We Do: We take educated risks. We take chances not because we are foolish but because we have prepared for the next level. We believe in ourselves and our abilities. We make things happen. We move forward on purpose for a purpose.

What We Don't Do: We don't take risks for the sake of taking risks. We don't gamble and take random chances. We don't attempt to move forward without preparing in advance.

Bad Example(s): Failing to pay the price to get to the next level. Failing to make the sacrifices that will take us to the next level. Being undisciplined and flowing with the current instead of charting our own course.

> **Think About This**
>
> "To grow, you must be willing to let your present and your future be totally unlike your past. Your history is not your destiny."
> ~ Alan Cohen

Ask Yourself: Do I truly believe in myself? What would others say? Why? What does my behavior reveal? Am I already intentionally traveling down a path I designed, or am I traveling down the path of chance and random opportunity?

What Do You Think?

SECTION 2

TOOLBOX TIPS BASED ON "BLUE-COLLAR LEADERSHIP® & TEAMWORK: 30 TRAITS OF HIGH IMPACT PLAYERS"

🔧 Toolbox Tip #31

We should be growth-oriented, not goal-oriented.

Why It Matters: Constant growth creates freedom and options. Life is always better with more freedom and more options. When we're goal-oriented, we may reach the goal and quit growing. When we quit growing, we should expect to be left behind by those who are still growing.

What We Do: When we're growth-oriented, we set goals that facilitate constant growth. When we reach a goal, we automatically set a new goal that will help us continue climbing to the next level and beyond.

What We Don't Do: We don't set a goal, reach it, and begin resting on our past growth. We don't go with the status quo. We don't rest on what we did 1, 5, 10, or 20 years ago. We don't coast.

Bad Example(s): We graduate high school or college and never read another book. We only grow when others require us to grow.

> ### Think About This
>
> "The vast majority of us now work in environments where the ability to learn is more critical than what we know and where the most valuable currency is influence, not power."
> ~ Liz Wiseman

Ask Yourself: If I'm not growth-oriented, how can I expect to compete with someone who is? Am I growth-oriented? Why or why not? How will this impact my career in the future?

What Do You Think?

🔧 Toolbox Tip #32

We should be trustworthy. Trust is based on two things: 1) our character (87%), who we are; and 2) our competency (13%), what we know.

Why It Matters: Trust is the foundation for authentic influence. Without trust, we will have no authentic influence with anyone at home or at work.

What We Do: We develop our character because our character will either launch us or limit us. We should always seek mutual benefit. We make choices that build trust and avoid choices that create distrust.

What We Don't Do: We don't do things that create distrust such as: talk behind someone's back, blame others, avoid taking responsibility, make and break commitments, and attempt to manipulate others.

Bad Example(s): We say we're going to do something, but then we don't. We make excuses for our bad behavior. We lie to others. We blame others and avoid responsibility.

> ### *Think About This*
>
> "Whoever is careless with the truth in small matters cannot be trusted with important matters." ~ Albert Einstein

Ask Yourself: How do I intentionally build trust with my teammates? How do I accidentally create distrust with my teammates? Do others see me seeking mutual benefit or personal benefit? Am I trustworthy?

What Do You Think?

🔧 Toolbox Tip #33

We should be humble. We don't want the spotlight shining on us. Instead, we intentionally try to shine it on others.

Why It Matters: Our level of humility reveals our level of security. Humility has nothing to do with position, title, and rank. Humility has everything to do with our character. Humble people can never be humiliated. People with too much pride and ego are easily humiliated.

What We Do: We must focus on developing our weaknesses relative to our character (who we are) because these weaknesses will turn confidence into arrogance. We give credit to others when things go right. We take the blame when things go wrong.

What We Don't Do: We don't seek attention. We don't take credit for another's idea or work. We don't think we're better than anyone else. We don't think anyone else is better than us. We don't seek the spotlight.

Bad Example(s): We accept credit for the work of another. We talk down to others or about others as if we are perfect and never make mistakes. We expect others to be perfect when we are not. We seek attention to appear *"better than"* the rest of our team.

> ### Think About This
>
> "Being humble doesn't mean you lack self-confidence, or you never stand up for your own opinions or principles. It does mean recognizing you don't know everything–and you're willing to learn from others." ~ Justin Bariso

Ask Yourself: Do I seek attention? If so, why? Do I take credit for what others have done, especially if I believe no one will discover the truth? If so, why? Do I blame others for making the same mistakes I make or have made? If so, why?

What Do You Think?

🔧 Toolbox Tip #34

We should be responsible. Each of us is responsible for choosing our values and those values will determine our circumstances and the impact we have, especially when it comes to teamwork. *Note: You can read the related chapter on page 144.*

Why It Matters: Making this choice gives us a voice. When we take responsibility, we gain influence related to what we are doing, how we do it, and what we will do next. High impact people know the quickest way to build trust with leaders or team member is to help them get results, so that's what they focus on doing.

What We Do: When low impact people start whining, we step up, take responsibility, and start shining. We get results while those who don't get overlooked. We help our team members get results. We help our leaders get results. We help the organization get results.

What We Don't Do: We don't dodge responsibility. We don't transfer our responsibilities. We don't wait for someone to tell us what to do. We don't wait for others to do what we already know should be done. We don't have a bad attitude when asked to step up. We don't expect our team to carry our load.

Bad Example(s): We know exactly what needs doing, but don't do it. We have the ability and time to take on more responsibility, but hope we don't get asked to step up. When asked to take on more responsibility, we attempt to talk our way out of it.

Think About This

"The degree to which you accept responsibility for everything in your life is precisely the degree of personal power you have to change or create anything in your life." ~ Hal Elrod

---

Ask Yourself: If I accept more responsibility, how will I benefit? Will I gain more experience? Will that experience make me more valuable to this organization or another organization? If I was a leader, how would I view those who dodge responsibility? Would they have more influence with me or less? Would I be more or less likely to value their opinions?

What Do You Think?

🔧 Toolbox Tip #35

We should be positive because our emotions can make or break us.

Why It Matters: Those who are whining get left behind by those who are shining. When it comes to teamwork, emotions matter a lot because emotions are contagious. Negativity is the most contagious emotion of all. A negative attitude is easy to catch and easy to spread.

What We Do: We choose to remain positive, especially in negative situations. When others are being negative, we help everyone look for and see the positive in the situation. We avoid expressing anger and frustration. We pause and choose our response based on values, not feelings. We choose to be positive while others are choosing to be negative. We lift others.

What We Don't Do: We don't get sucked into the whirlpool of negativity when it forms. We don't join the whiners who are contaminating our team with toxic, morale killing negativity. We don't tear others down.

Bad Example(s): We publicly offer support to our team and our leader, but we privately do and say negative things that undermine our team members, our leaders, and ultimately our organization. We hear something we don't like and instantly let anger and frustration start flowing from our mouths.

> ### Think About This
>
> "Real optimism is aware of problems but recognizes solutions; knows about difficulties but believes they can be overcome; sees the negatives, but accentuates the positives; is exposed to the worst but expects the best; has reason to complain, but chooses to smile."
> ~ William Arthur Ward

Ask Yourself: If I'm leading a team, do I prefer to have positive team members or negative? Why does it matter? Am I a positive or negative team member? What impact does my attitude have on my influence with others? Do I have more influence with positive people if I'm being negative? Are those who attempt to pull me down with negativity helping me or harming me? Do they have my best interest in mind?

What Do You Think?

🔧 *Toolbox Tip #36*

We should be flexible because change happens.

Why It Matters: Change is the norm, not the exception. All of our growth happens beyond our comfort zone. When change happens, some team members will thrive while other team members take a dive. Those leading change are looking for help not roadblocks.

What We Do: We intentionally embrace change. We support change. We leverage change for our benefit. We lead change. We look for ways to improve our processes because our ability to change quickly is a competitive advantage. High impact people are change champions.

What We Don't Do: We don't resist or avoid change which only provides our competition with a huge competitive advantage. We don't become negative when change happens. We don't resist or avoid change because doing so doesn't help us advance; it ensures we won't.

Bad Example(s): We learn that something is changing. Instead of jumping on board and offering information and ideas to help implement the change in an effective way, we simply start telling everyone who will listen why it's a bad idea and why it'll never work.

> ### Think About This
>
> "If you don't like change, you're going to like irrelevance even less." ~ General Eric Shinseki

Ask Yourself: If I am responsible for leading change, do I want a team of people around me that will help me be more effective or more ineffective? If I want to compete for promotions and pay raises, should I focus on shining or whining? If everyone around me is whining and I'm shining, will my influence increase or decrease? Will I have more options with more or less influence?

What Do You Think?

🔧 Toolbox Tip #37

We should be focused because minimizing our distractions maximizes our results.

Why It Matters. Our ability to deliver results will determine the job we have, the pay we earn, the impact we have, and the life we live.

What We Do: We live with purpose. We play to win instead of playing not to lose. We do more than is required. We live life by design, not by accident. We chart our own course.

What We Don't Do: We don't let others distract us from our mission. We don't do only what's required, or worse, less than is required. We don't blame others for our circumstances.

Bad Example(s): We take any good paying job we're offered because we haven't been intentional about taking responsibility for developing ourselves to get the job we want. We're not happy with our life at work and/or at home and blame others for our misery.

> ### Think About This
>
> "Winners concentrate on winning.
> Losers concentrate on getting by."
> ~ Truett Cathy

Ask Yourself: When I look in the mirror, do I see someone living life by design or by accident? Am I even focused on my future? Am I where I am today because this is where I wanted to be at this time in my life? Or, did I simply go with the flow and end up here? What's truly stopping me from focusing on preparing myself for a better future?

What Do You Think?

🔧 Toolbox Tip #38

We should be disciplined. The greater the discipline, the better the person. When we have discipline, we give ourselves a command and follow through. Our words matter.

Why It Matters: Making commitments creates hope. Keeping commitments builds trust. Breaking commitments creates distrust. Trust is the foundation of authentic influence. Increasing your influence increases your options.

What We Do: We think before we make commitments. We do what we said we would do, when we said we would do it, how we said we would do it, because we said we would do it. If we can't keep a commitment, we ask to be released from our promise.

What We Don't Do: We don't make commitments lightly. We don't break commitments once we make them. We don't stand people up. We don't change our mind and leave others hanging.

Bad Example(s): We tell someone we will meet them at a certain time, but we show up late. We tell someone we will do something, but we never do it. We tell someone we will do something a certain way, but we do it a different way. We say one thing and do another.

> ### Think About This
>
> "The pain of discipline weighs ounces. Regret weighs tons." ~ Jim Rohn

Ask Yourself: How often do I make and break commitments? At work? At home? How do I feel when someone makes a commitment to me but doesn't follow through? Do I trust them more or less? Do I think before making commitments? When I break a commitment, do I consider how I put myself into a situation of creating distrust? How can I improve in this area?

What Do You Think?

🔧 *Toolbox Tip #39*

We should be intentional. Being disciplined is closely related to being intentional. However, these are two very different traits. Being disciplined is about making and keeping commitments to ourselves and to others. Being intentional is about making and keeping commitments related to specific goals or objectives

Why It Matters: Actions today lead to options tomorrow. Our future is created daily, not in a day. We can't predict our future, but we can absolutely create it by living intentionally.

What We Do: We evaluate who we are and where we are. We determine who we want to be and where we want to be. We then become intentional about our choices. We constantly ask, *"Will what I'm about to do move me in the right direction?"* If yes, we do it. If no, we don't do it.

What We Don't Do: We don't moan and groan about where we are or what we're doing. We don't settle for remaining the same in a changing world. We don't wait for others to develop us. We don't hope and wish for a better life or a better job. We don't coast. We don't settle.

Bad Example(s): We don't have a plan to get from

where we are to where we want to be. We don't lead ourselves well, but we blame others for not leading us well. We don't grow through life, we go through life.

> **Think About This**
>
> "If you don't lead yourself intentionally, you'll be led by others automatically."
> ~ Mack Story

Ask Yourself: Am I intentional with my time? Do I waste my time when I'm not at work? Or, do I invest my time when I'm not at work? Are my activities away from work moving me closer to the future I desire or ensuring very little changes? What's stopping me from becoming more intentional? Is my behavior aligned with my goals and my vision of the future? What needs to change? How can I become more intentional?

What Do You Think?

BlueCollarLeadership.com

 *Toolbox Tip #40*

We should be driven by our purpose.

Why It Matters: When we're on a team, we can be "*starters*" or "*bench warmers.*" The starters get noticed. The bench warmers get overlooked. The starters get opportunities. The bench warmers get passed by. The starters determine their future. The bench warmers hope and wish for a better future.

What We Do: We consistently and constantly develop ourselves. We become people who CAN influence our teammates because of our results. We become people who are WILLING TO influence our teammates because of our character.

What We Don't Do: We don't stand in the shadows. We don't play small when we're capable of playing tall. We don't watch others pass us by. We don't make excuses for being overlooked. We don't blame those who have put in the work when they pass us.

Bad Example(s): When we're overlooked for a promotion, we become angry and frustrated blaming everyone but ourselves. We won't develop ourselves but become angry at those who do. We choose to waste our time instead of investing our time.

> ### Think About This
>
> "Success bases our worth on a comparison with others. Excellence gauges our value by measuring us against our own potential."
> ~ John Johnson

Ask Yourself: Do I want to be a starter or a bench warmer? What does my behavior and choices reveal? Are my actions aligned with the words I speak? What would a driven person do in my situation? Am I doing that? Have I been passed by? If so, what should I have done to prevent that from happening?

What Do You Think?

🔧 Toolbox Tip #41

We should be Inspired. If we don't go within, we will go without.

Why It Matters: If we're not inspired, we are depending on others to motivate us into action. If no one motivates us, we simply coast. We won't get very far in life if we coast.

What We Do: We lead ourselves well. We find methods to motivate ourselves. We read motivational and inspirational books, listen to audios, and watch videos. We invest our time and resources in our own personal development. We share what we're learning with others.

What We Don't Do: We don't wait for someone else to motivate and inspire us. We don't wait for others to take the time to develop us. We don't wait for others to use their resources to develop us. We don't wait on anything.

Bad Example(s): We wish our leaders would invest in our development and get angry and frustrated when they don't. Yet, we don't invest in and develop ourselves. We blame others for not investing in us when we won't invest in ourselves. If we won't invest in ourselves, why should anyone else?

> ### *Think About This*
>
> "What stands between you and your goal is your behavior." ~ Darren Hardy

Ask Yourself: Am I inspired to climb to the next level and beyond? Or, am I happy leaving my future in someone else's hands? What does my behavior reveal? Am I fooling myself? Do I blame others for holding me back when it's really me who is doing the most damage? What inspires me? If I'm not inspired to get better, why not?

What Do You Think?

🔧 Toolbox Tip #42

We should be proud and exhibit confidence without arrogance.

Why It Matters. If we don't take pride in our work, others will question our ability to perform at a high level. If others believe we can't perform at a high level, we may miss opportunities.

What We Do: We ask for feedback. We get results. We produce high quality work. We work well with others. We support others. We share knowledge and information. We have confidence in our abilities. We make things happen. We strive for success. We remain proud but humble.

What We Don't Do: We don't belittle others. We don't point out the shortcomings of others. We don't brag about our abilities and accomplishments. We don't hoard knowledge and information. We don't act or speak in an arrogant manner. We don't appear to be cocky.

Bad Example(s): We perform well and make sure everyone knows it. We brag about ourselves while badmouthing others. Instead of completing our teammates, we compete with our teammates.

> ### *Think About This*
>
> "You will never get to the next level if you can't
> embrace feedback about your performance
> at the current level." ~ Henry Cloud

Ask Yourself: Do others see me as confident? Or, cocky and arrogant? How do I feel about those who I see as arrogant and cocky? Do I respect them? Do I trust them? What can I do to ensure I'm seen as confident but not cocky? What behavior should I adopt? What behavior should I drop?

What Do You Think?

🔧 *Toolbox Tip #43*

We should be brave because courage is contagious. Courage allows average people to achieve exceptional results.

Why It Matters: It often takes courage to do the right things for the right reasons at the right time in the right way.

What We Do: We live with integrity. We take action when others don't or won't. We seek mutual benefit. We focus on doing what's right, not on being right.

What We Don't Do: We don't moan and groan in the shadows. We don't tell others what they should do. We don't expect someone else to do what we could and should be doing.

Bad Example(s): Being the first one on the team to point out what should be done while doing nothing. Being the loudest voice on the team when the boss isn't around while remaining silent when the boss asks for suggestions. Complaining about what isn't being done while doing nothing.

Think About This

"Within every organization in need of change, there is a group of insiders who are keenly aware of the transformations that need to take place. They go home every night and gripe to their spouses. They gather in the break room and complain to each other. But day after day, they go about their work resigned to the notion that nothing will change. They are convinced that to try to introduce change would be a costly — and potentially hazardous — waste of time. So, they keep their mouth shut and watch the clock. They don't lack insight into what needs to happen; they simply lack the courage to do anything about it."
~ Andy Stanley

Ask Yourself: What would change if I had more courage? Where in my life is a lack of courage holding me back? Do I truly have the courage to stand alone when necessary? What does my behavior reveal? Does my team see me as brave or cowardly? Who earns more respect a brave person or a coward? Which would I trust more? Which has more influence?

What Do You Think?

🔧 Toolbox Tip #44

We should be teachable and embrace a beginner's mindset.

Why It Matters: We don't know what we don't know. If we come across as a know-it-all, people are more likely to withhold information. We will never know it all. No one will. Only the arrogant among us act as if they know it all.

What We Do: We seek constant growth. We listen with the intent to learn. We seek knowledge from multiple sources. We understand that everyone we meet knows something we don't. We remain curious. We often ask, *"Why?"* or *"How?"*

What We Don't Do: We don't assume we know everything there is to know, no matter how old we are or how long we've been doing our job. We don't assume what we learned yesterday, last week, or last year still applies today. We don't overlook the knowledge a new team member has.

Bad Example(s): Choosing to ignore the input of someone because they are young or new to the job. Brushing aside improvement suggestions by team members, especially new or young team members. Not listening to those closest to the problem when we're trying to solve a problem.

> ### Think About This
>
> "There are some people that if they don't know, you can't tell them." ~ Louis Armstrong

Ask Yourself: Do I seek input from young, new, or inexperienced team members? If not, why not? Am I curious about learning? Or, do I expect what I learned in the past to carry me into the future? If the world is changing every day, how can I remain the same? What do I need to learn?

What Do You Think?

🔧 Toolbox Tip #45

We should be open-minded because there's always another way.

Why It Matters: High impact people don't simply look for a solution to a problem. They look for the best solution. They leverage the minds of all the people on their team. They know these truths: None of us is as smart as all of us. None of us is as creative as all of us.

What We Do: We open new doors in new places. We do new things. We do old things in new ways. We remain curious. We ask lots of questions. We meet new people. We share ideas and seek out new ideas. We learn from multiple sources. We aim to complete our teammates, not to compete with our teammates. We leverage multiple minds instead of just our own.

What We Don't Do: We don't attempt to learn from only a few sources. We don't think our way is the only way. We don't think our way is always the right way. We don't limit input from others.

Bad Example(s): When we're working on a project and someone offers a suggestion, we don't slow down to consider it or why the suggestion was made in the first place. We refuse to listen to those who think different than we do.

> ### Think About This
>
> "Mindset change is not about picking up a few pointers here and there. It's about seeing things in a new way." ~ Carol S. Dweck

Ask Yourself: Do I ever reject input from others? Do I resist learning from people who aren't like me? Can I disagree with someone in one area but learn from them in another area? Have I been limiting myself by rejecting others ideas based on their age, background, education? How do I feel when others won't listen to me? If I don't listen to others, am I any different than those who won't listen to me?

What Do You Think?

🔧 Toolbox Tip #46

We should be approachable because who we know determines where we go.

Why It Matters: We can't accomplish very much alone. We can't expect someone to help us if they don't know us. We can't help others if we don't know them.

What We Do: We intentionally build relationships with others. When others approach us, we listen with the intent to understand. We live life with a positive attitude. We aren't afraid to smile. We go out of our way to interact with others.

What We Don't Do: We don't walk around with a chip on our shoulder. We don't make rude or belittling comments to others or about others. We don't raise our voice or roll our eyes when we don't like what we're hearing. We don't avoid others. We don't give short incomplete answers.

Bad Example(s): When people attempt to talk to us, we take over the conversation. We don't listen to understand but rather with the intent to reply. We don't ask questions. We simply want to be understood. We don't attempt to make a real connection. We don't share information.

> ### *Think About This*
>
> "My success, personally and professionally, is based on my ability to connect and communicate. And, so is yours." ~ Ria Story

Ask Yourself: Do others see me as approachable? Do a lot of people speak to me? If so, what am I doing right? Do most people avoid me? If so, why? If people are avoiding me, do I have more influence or less? How can people help me if they don't know me?

What Do You Think?

… Toolbox Tip #47

We should be helpful because what we do reveals who we are.

Why It Matters. Everyone is watching. The more helpful we become, the more valuable we become. The more valuable we become, the more successful we become.

What We Do: We look for opportunities to help our teammates, our leaders, and our family. We sacrifice time and energy to help others. We do little things that make a big difference. We know it's not about us, but it does start with us.

What We Don't Do: We don't wait for others to ask for help. We don't wait for someone to need our help. We don't hope they ask someone else. We don't wait for someone else to help.

Bad Example(s): Knowing someone needs our help, but we don't offer our help. Being asked to help but refusing to help. Avoiding people who may need our help.

> **Think About This**
>
> "A hero is someone you idolize, while a mentor is someone you respect. A hero earns our amazement; a mentor earns our confidence. A hero takes our breath away; a mentor is given our trust. Mentors do not seek to create a new person; they simply seek to help a person become a better version of himself."
> ~ John Wooden

Ask Yourself: How can I be more intentional about helping my team? When others help me, how do I feel? When others refuse to help me, how do I feel? Who has more influence, those who help others or those who don't?

What Do You Think?

🔧 Toolbox Tip #48

We should be observant because with people the little things are often the big things.

Why It Matters: The first person to help is always acknowledged. The first to help quickly builds trust. The first to help gains the most influence.

What We Do: We pay attention to those around us. We look for opportunities to help. We focus on the needs of others. We shift the focus from ourselves to others.

What We Don't Do: We don't keep to ourselves. We don't wander through the world as if we are the only people who matter. We don't miss an opportunity to leverage our strengths and experience.

Bad Example(s): Waiting until someone needs our help to offer our help. Knowing we should help someone but pretending we are unaware of their need.

> ### Think About This
>
> "A basic truth of life is that people will always move toward anyone who increases them and away from those who devalue them."
> ~ John C. Maxwell

Ask Yourself: How do I feel when I need help and others offer their assistance before I ask for it? Does the relationship get stronger or weaker as a result? How often do I observe others needing help without choosing to help? Am I going to be more successful if I'm more observant or less observant?

What Do You Think?

🔧 Toolbox Tip #49

We should be engaged because engagement leads to involvement.

Why It Matters. Those who are the most engaged have the most influence. Those who are the least engaged have the least influence.

What We Do: We do more than required. We do things sooner than required. We do things better than required. We do the things others don't want to do. We take ownership. We find a way to deliver results.

What We Don't Do: We don't do less than required. We don't do things later than required. We don't leave things unfinished. We don't transfer our responsibilities to others. We don't make excuses when we fail to produce the desired results.

Bad Example(s): Saying any of the following…"That's not my job," "Sorry, I forgot to tell you," "That's above my pay grade," "I'm just here for the pay," "They don't pay me to think," "That's not my responsibility," "I didn't know. No one told me," "How is it my fault? I didn't know," "If they would have told me sooner," "I'm just here to do my eight and hit the gate," "You should have known I needed to know."

Think About This

"I am responsible for taking action, asking questions, getting answers, and making decisions. I won't wait for someone to tell me. If I need to know, I'm responsible for asking. I have no right to be offended that I didn't *get this sooner.* If I'm doing something others should know about, I'm responsible for telling them." ~ Garry Ridge, CEO WD-40

Ask Yourself: How engaged am I? How much more engaged could I be? Is my lack of engagement holding me back? What would change if I became more engaged? What would those on my team say if I became more engaged? Would they support me? If so, what does that mean? Would they make fun of me? If so, what does that mean?

What Do You Think?

🔧 Toolbox Tip #50

We should be present and look for the golden nuggets of wisdom that are all around us.

Why It Matters: The key to a better life is intentional growth and development, not luck. The more we grow, the farther we go. High impact people live life on purpose, personally and professionally.

What We Do: We do everything with purpose. We walk with purpose. We talk with purpose. We work with purpose. We live with purpose. When it comes to life, we are fully present.

What We Don't Do: We don't expect to get something for nothing. We don't wait for luck to come our way. We don't hang around people who are going nowhere. We don't let others hold us back. We don't miss an opportunity to learn.

Bad Example(s): Having someone invest time to help you grow and develop but not appreciating it. Having someone give you a book but not reading it. Listening to a speaker or trainer provide you with valuable information but not absorbing it or taking action.

> ### *Think About This*
>
> "If I read a book that cost me $20 and I get one good idea, I've gotten one of the greatest bargains of all time." ~ Tom Peters

Ask Yourself: Am I looking to mine the golden nuggets in this lesson? Do I appreciate my leaders investing time and money in my development? If yes, have I thanked them? If not, why not? If I don't appreciate it, why should they keep investing in me? What message do I send if I'm engaged? If I'm not engaged? Are pride and ego preventing me from mining the golden nuggets?

What Do You Think?

🔧 Toolbox Tip #51

We should be understanding which means we seek to understand what others are seeing, feeling, and experiencing before we seek to be understood.

Why It Matters: The key to influencing others is to allow them to influence us first. When others feel understood, they are open to trying to understand us. But, if others don't feel understood, they won't be listening to understand. Instead, they will be listening with the intent to reply in an effort to get us to understand them.

What We Do: We squint with our eyes to see the emotions wrapped around words. We squint with our ears to hear meaning hidden between words. We attempt to fully understand before attempting to be understood. We allow others to go first.

What We Don't Do: We don't listen with the intent to reply. We don't keep typing on our device when someone is talking to us. We don't keep working while someone is talking to us. We don't attempt to go first.

Bad Example(s): Saying we understand although the other person clearly doesn't feel understood. Cutting others off to speed up the conversation. Nodding but not listening...waiting to reply.

> ### Think About This
>
> "Educating the mind without educating the heart is no education at all." ~ Aristotle

Ask Yourself: Do I listen to understand or to reply? Can I tell when others are truly listening to me? How do I feel when they do? How do I feel when they don't? Where do I need to improve the most? At home? At work? When I don't listen, why don't I?

What Do You Think?

🔧 Toolbox Tip #52

We should be competent because trust is based not only on character (87%) but also on competency (13%).

Why It Matters: Our character multiplies our competency. Without competency, we may be able to build relationships, but we can't achieve any meaningful results.

What We Do: We leverage our competency strengths and ignore our competency weaknesses. Our competency strength is where we will excel with intentional development. We leverage our character strengths and develop our character weaknesses. Our character weaknesses will hold us back like an anchor and limit us regardless of our competency.

What We Don't Do: We don't attempt to develop our competency weaknesses because they're weaknesses for a reason. We're not naturally good in that area. We don't spend a lot of time and energy focusing on areas where we're not naturally talented.

Bad Example(s): Educating ourselves in the area of competency but failing to do the necessary character work to get the benefit of our competency. Being a brilliant jerk that no one wants to work with.

> **Think About This**
>
> "CHARACTER + (the appropriate) COMPETENCY = TRUST"
> ~ Mack Story

Ask Yourself: Is my character higher than my competency? If so, my character will multiply my competency. Is my competency higher than my character? If so, my lack of character development is holding me back whether I know it or not. Do I intentionally develop my character and my competency? When I think about climbing to the next level, do I think of developing my character and my competency?

What Do You Think?

🔧 Toolbox Tip #53

We should be certain because our integrity is on the line.

Why It Matters: Every time we open our mouth we are putting our integrity to the test. If we speak with certainty based on truth, we strengthen our integrity. If we speak with certainty but don't know if what we're saying is true or false, we risk our integrity. If we speak with certainty and know what we're saying is false, we weaken our integrity.

What We Do: We only speak the truth. We confirm the rumor before we consider spreading the rumor. We value our credibility and integrity more than we value spreading unverified information.

What We Don't Do: We don't spread misinformation. We don't believe everything we hear. We don't assume something is true just because we heard a leader say it. We don't assume something is true just because everyone is saying it. We don't assume something is true because we heard it from a friend. We don't share what we think is true, only what we know to be true.

Bad Example(s): We come to work, hear a rumor, and start telling others what we've heard without confirming if it's actually true. Someone tells us they heard or read something, and we start telling others as if it's true although we haven't confirmed it to be true. Our boss tells us why things are the way they are, so we start telling others assuming the boss knows, but the boss doesn't know; and what we were told was a guess and wasn't true.

> ### *Think About This*
>
> "I look for three things in hiring people. The first is personal integrity, the second is intelligence, and the third is a high energy level. But, if you don't have the first, the other two will kill you."
> ~ Warren Buffet

Ask Yourself: Do I speak without verifying what I'm saying? Do I read something on social media and spread it as the truth? Do I spread gossip at work? Do I value my integrity more than I value being seen as *"in the know?"* How do I feel when others tell me a lie? Why would I tell someone a lie?

What Do You Think?

🔧 Toolbox Tip #54

We should be motivational because motivation leads to inspiration.

Why It Matters: Doing a great job is one thing, but motivating others to do a great job is something completely different. Those who can motivate others to do a great job are much more valuable than those who can't.

What We Do: We seek mutual benefit. We want to win, but we also want everyone else on our team to win. We make choices and behave in ways that build trust. We lead by example. We believe in our team.

What We Don't Do: We don't attempt to manipulate others for personal gain. We don't take actions that only benefit us. We don't create distrust.

Bad Example(s): We expect others to do what we're unwilling to do. We ignore everyone else and do what's best for us without caring how it impacts the rest of the team. We grandstand and take the credit for the success of the team.

Think About This

"Coaches that can outline plays on a blackboard are a dime a dozen, but the ones that can succeed are the ones that can get inside their players and motivate them."
~ Vince Lombardi

Ask Yourself: When making a decision, do I pause and consider the impact it will have on the team? What do my teammates do that motivates me? Do I do those things? Why or why not? Am I more focused on getting ahead or helping others get ahead? What does my answer say about my character? Am I more valuable if I can get ahead by myself or if I can help others on my team get ahead?

What Do You Think?

🔧 *Toolbox Tip #55*

We should be **inspirational** because inspiration leads to appreciation.

Why It Matters: When we inspire others to get better, they appreciate us. When others appreciate us, they support us. When we help others get results, they are more likely to help us get results.

What We Do: We do the hard job without complaining. We have a positive attitude when others are negative. We go the extra mile for our teammates. We carry more than our fair share of the load. We build trust instead of creating distrust. We grow and develop ourselves with the intent of growing and developing others, at home and at work. We accept more than our fair share of the blame when things go wrong.

What We Don't Do: We don't think we're special. We don't seek credit. We don't expect others to carry our load. We don't wait until we have a leadership position before we start leading.

Bad Example(s): Having a *"me"* frame of reference instead of a *"we"* frame of reference. Speaking highly of yourself instead of highly of your team. Doing the easy work and leaving the hard work for someone else. Expecting someone else to clean up your mess.

> ### Think About This
>
> "There is always a choice about the way you do your work, even if there is not a choice about the work itself."
> ~ Lundin, Paul, & Christensen

Ask Yourself: What type of behavior inspires me? Do I exhibit that type of behavior? If not, why not? When was the last time a teammate inspired me? When was the last time I inspired a teammate? Can my team count on me to do the right thing even when no one is looking? When was the last time someone told me I inspired them?

What Do You Think?

🔧 Toolbox Tip #56

We should be aware because we can't beware until we're aware.

Why It Matters. Our lack of awareness is holding us back whether we know it or not and whether we believe it or not. We all have a blind spot, and it's in the same place: between us and the mirror.

What We Do: We ask for and encourage feedback from our teammates, leaders, and family. We seek intentional growth to raise our awareness. We assume we have blind spots.

What We Don't Do: We don't assume we know it all. We don't assume we don't have blind spots. We don't get defensive when others offer feedback whether we ask for it or not. We don't always assume everything that goes wrong in our lives is someone else's fault.

Bad Example(s): We don't feel like we have to grow. We feel as though everything that's wrong in our life is someone else's fault, especially our boss, our spouse, and our children. We refuse to take ownership for our role in negative situations.

> ### *Think About This*
>
> "You can't make the other person feel important in your presence if you secretly feel they are a nobody." ~ Les Giblin

Ask Yourself: Is my lack of awareness holding me back? How would I know? When things go wrong, is my first reaction to instantly blame others? Or, is my reaction to pause and look in the mirror to see how I contributed to the situation?

What Do You Think?

🔧 Toolbox Tip #57

We should be careful because some people would rather tear us down than lift us up.

Why It Matters: Not everyone has the same values. When it comes to values, those who are most like you like you the most. Those who are least like you like you the least.

What We Do: We intentionally avoid toxic relationships, at home and at work. If an existing relationship becomes toxic, we have the courage to end it. We don't let toxic people pull us down to their level. We maintain control of ourselves and make our choices based on our values.

What We Don't Do: We don't think we're better than anyone else. We don't lose control. We don't allow toxic people to negatively influence us. We don't associate with those who are trying to pull us down or prevent us from climbing to the next level and beyond.

Bad Example(s): Trusting everyone unconditionally. Assuming everyone has your best interests in mind, especially your boss or spouse. Thinking everyone has the same intentions as you.

> ### *Think About This*
>
> "The moment there is suspicion about a person's motives, everything he does becomes tainted." ~ Mahatma Gandhi

Ask Yourself: Who do I trust the most in my personal life? Why? Who do I trust the most in my professional life? Why? When have I been burned by someone I trusted? Did I miss the red flags? Or, did I ignore them? What role did I play? How could I have prevented it?

What Do You Think?

🔧 *Toolbox Tip #58*

We should be optimistic. Hope isn't a strategy, but it's needed to develop one.

Why It Matters: Without a positive outlook on the future, we won't develop a strategy for our future. Without hope for a better future, we won't work hard to create that future. Hope alone won't get you to the next level. But, hope will help you get to the next level.

What We Do: We believe tomorrow can and should be better. We believe we can and should be better. We believe our teammates can and should be better. We believe our organization can and should be better. We have a preferred vision for our future.

What We Don't Do: We don't dwell on the negative. We don't associate with negative people. We don't listen to or watch negative news, listen to negative audio, or read negative articles. We don't allow toxic people to cloud our vision.

Bad Example(s): We look for the bad in every situation instead of the good. We expect the worst from people instead of the best. We maintain relationships long after we know we should have ended them because we have false hope.

> ### *Think About This*
>
> *Thinking* by Walter D. Wintle, "If you think you are beaten, you are. If you think you dare not, you don't. If you like to win but you think you can't, it is almost certain you won't. If you think you'll lose, you've lost. For out of the world, we find success begins with a fellow's will. It's all in the state of mind. If you think you're outclassed, you are. You've got to think high to rise. You've got to be sure of yourself before you can ever win a prize. Life's battles don't always go to the stronger or faster man. But sooner or later, the man who wins is the man who thinks he can."

Ask Yourself: Do I believe I can truly transform my life? Do I believe I should? Do I believe I can contribute at a higher level? Do I believe I should? Do I believe I can help my family get better? Do I believe I should? Am I involved in toxic relationships that are holding me back? What's stopping me from taking action?

What Do You Think?

 Toolbox Tip #59

We should be realistic because we are exactly where our values have led us. If we were supposed to be someplace else in life, we would already be there.

Why It Matters: Our values are the foundation for our circumstances. Our values determine our thoughts which cause our feelings. Our feelings influence our choices which lead to our results. Our results determine our circumstances.

What We Do: We accept responsibility for our circumstances. We choose our values. We make our choices; then, our choices make us. We understand change may only be temporary, but personal transformation is more likely to be permanent. We know taking responsibility for our circumstances means we can change our circumstances. We hit the reset button when necessary.

What We Don't Do: We don't throw pity parties for ourselves. We don't blame others for our circumstances. We don't expect anyone else to change our circumstances.

Bad Example(s): Thinking that a new boss is going to make your life better. Thinking that a new job will make your life better. Thinking that a raise will make your life better. Thinking your life will get better without changing your values.

> **Think About This**
>
> "If Bob has a problem everywhere Bob goes, Bob is the problem." ~ unknown

Ask Yourself: What are my core values? Do I even know? Have I ever even thought about it? Am I exactly where I want to be in life doing what I want to be doing? If not, what values do I need to change? Am I happy at work? If not, what values do I need to change? Am I happy at home? If not, what values do I need to change?

What Do You Think?

🔧 Toolbox Tip #60

We should be relentless because until we quit, we haven't failed.

Why It Matters. Becoming a high impact individual isn't easy. It's hard! Transformation doesn't happen in a day. It happens daily.

What We Do: We intentionally move forward on purpose for a purpose. We intentionally do something every day to get better. We measure ourselves against our potential, not our peers.

What We Don't Do: We don't allow others to hold us back. We don't allow the negative opinions of others to slow us down. We don't give up, and we don't give in. We don't let the fear of failure hold us back.

Bad Example(s): Quitting when it gets hard. Thinking life will simply get better with very little intentional effort. Waiting to get started. Hoping and wishing instead of deciding and doing. Doing what everyone else is doing to get ahead, which is usually very little. Keeping the same values and expecting things to change.

Blue-Collar Leadership® Toolbox Tips

> ### *Think About This*
>
> "If we succeed, it will not be because of what we have, but it will be because of what we are; not because of what we own, but rather because of what we believe."
> ~ Lyndon B. Johnson

Ask Yourself: What's the most important thing I need to do? The one thing that if I don't do it nothing else matters? Why haven't I already done it? What's stopping me from doing it? What values are holding me back? When will I take action? What's one thing I can start doing every day to get a little better slowly and methodically?

What Do You Think?

I welcome hearing how this book has influenced the way you think, the way you lead, or the results you have achieved because of what you've learned in it. Please feel free to share your thoughts with me by email at:

Mack@MackStory.com

To learn more about my books, audiobooks, podcast, etc., please visit: BlueCollarLeadership.com or TopStoryLeadership.com

ABOUT THE AUTHOR

Mack's story is an amazing journey of personal and professional growth. He married Ria in 2001. He has one son, Eric, born in 1991.

After graduating high school in 1987, Mack joined the United States Marine Corps Reserve as an 0311 infantryman. Soon after, he began his 20 plus year manufacturing career. Graduating with highest honors, he earned an Executive Bachelor of Business Administration degree from Faulkner University.

Mack began his career in manufacturing in 1988 on the front lines of a large production machine shop. He eventually grew himself into upper management and found his niche in lean manufacturing and along with it, developed his passion for leadership. In 2008, he launched his own Lean Manufacturing and Leadership Development firm.

From 2005-2012, Mack led leaders and their cross-functional teams through more than 11,000 hours of process improvement, organizational change, and cultural transformation. Ria joined Mack full-time in late 2013.

In 2013, they worked with John C. Maxwell as part of an international training event focused on the Cultural Transformation in Guatemala where over 20,000 leaders were trained. They also shared the stage with internationally recognized motivational speaker Les Brown in 2014.

Mack and Ria have published 30+ books on personal growth and leadership development. In 2018, they were invited to speak at Yale University's School of Management. They also had over 80,000 international followers at the end of 2019 on LinkedIn where they provide daily motivational, inspirational, and leadership content to people around the world.

Mack and Ria inspire people everywhere through their example of achievement, growth, and personal development.

Clients: ATD (Association for Talent Development), Auburn University, Chevron, Chick-fil-A, Kimberly Clark, Koch Industries, Southern Company, and the U.S. Military.

WHAT WE OFFER:

- ✓ Keynote Speaking: Conferences, Seminars, Onsite
- ✓ Workshops: Onsite/Offsite Half/Full/Multi Day
- ✓ Leadership Development Support: Leadership, Teamwork, Personal Growth, Organizational Change, Planning, Executing, Trust, Cultural Transformation, Communication, Time Management, Selling with Character, Resilience, & Relationship Building
- ✓ Blue-Collar Leadership® Development
- ✓ Corporate Retreats
- ✓ Women's Retreat (with Ria Story)
- ✓ Limited one-on-one coaching/mentoring
- ✓ On-site Lean Leadership Certification
- ✓ Lean Leader Leadership Development
- ✓ Become licensed to teach our content

FOR MORE INFORMATION PLEASE VISIT:

BlueCollarLeadership.com
RiaStory.com
TopStoryLeadership.com

FOLLOW US ON SOCIAL MEDIA:

LinkedIn.com/in/MackStory
Facebook.com/Mack.Story

LinkedIn.com/in/RiaStory
Facebook.com/Ria.Story

LISTEN/SUBSCRIBE TO OUR PODCASTS AT:

TopStoryLeadership.com/podcast

Excerpt from

Defining Influence:
Increasing Your Influence Increases Your Options

In *Defining Influence*, I outline the foundational leadership principles and lessons we must learn in order to develop our character in a way that allows us to increase our influence with others. I also share many of my personal stories revealing how I got it wrong many times in the past and how I grew from front-line factory worker to become a Motivational Leadership Speaker.

INTRODUCTION

When You Increase Your Influence, You Increase Your Options.

"Leadership is influence. Nothing more. Nothing less. Everything rises and falls on leadership." ~ John C. Maxwell

Everyone is born a leader. However, everyone is not born a high impact leader.

I haven't always believed everyone is a leader. You may or may not at this point. That's okay. There is a lot to learn about leadership.

At this very moment, you may already be thinking to yourself, *"I'm not a leader."* My goal is to help you understand why everyone is a leader and to help you develop a deeper understanding of the principles of leadership and influence.

Developing a deep understanding of leadership has changed my life for the better. It has also changed the lives of my family members, friends, associates, and clients. My intention is to help you improve not only your life, but also the lives of those around you.

Until I became a student of leadership in 2008 which eventually led me to become a John Maxwell Certified Leadership Coach, Trainer, and Speaker in 2012, I did not understand leadership or realize everyone can benefit from learning the related principles.

In the past, I thought leadership was a term associated with being the boss and having formal authority over others. Those people are definitely leaders. But, I had been missing something. All of the other seven billion people on the planet are leaders too.

I say everyone is born a leader because I agree with John Maxwell, *"Leadership is Influence. Nothing more. Nothing less."* Everyone has influence. It's a fact. Therefore, everyone is a leader.

No matter your age, gender, religion, race, nationality, location, or position, everyone has influence. Whether you want to be a leader or not, you are. After reading this book, I hope you do not question whether or not you are a leader. However, I do hope you question what type of leader you are and what you need to do to increase your influence.

Everyone does not have authority, but everyone does have influence. There are plenty of examples in the world of people without authority leading people through influence alone. Actually, every one of us is an example. We have already done it. We know it is true. This principle is self-evident which means it contains its own evidence and does not need to be demonstrated or explained; it is obvious to everyone: we all have influence with others.

As I mentioned, the question to ask yourself is not, *"Am I a leader?"* The question to ask yourself is, *"What type of leader am I?"* The answer: whatever kind you choose to be. Choosing not to be a leader is not an option. As long as you live, you will have influence. You are a leader.

You started influencing your parents before you were actually born. You may have influence after your death. How? Thomas Edison still influences the world every time a light is turned on. You may do things in your life to influence others long after you're gone. Or, you may pass away with few people noticing. It depends on the choices you make.

Even when you're alone, you have influence.

The most important person you will ever influence is yourself. The degree to which you influence yourself determines the level of influence you ultimately have with others. Typically, when we are talking about leading ourselves, the word most commonly used to describe self-leadership is discipline which can be defined as giving yourself a command and following through with it. We must practice discipline daily to increase our influence with others.

> *"We must all suffer one of two things: the pain of discipline or the pain of regret or disappointment." ~ Jim Rohn*

As I define leadership as influence, keep in mind the words leadership and influence can be interchanged anytime and anywhere. They are one and the same. Throughout this book, I'll help you remember by placing one of the words in parentheses next to the other occasionally as a reminder. They are synonyms. When you read one, think of the other.

Everything rises and falls on influence (leadership). When you share what you're learning, clearly define leadership as influence for others. They need to understand the context of what you are teaching and understand they *are* leaders (people with influence) too. If you truly want to learn and apply leadership principles, you must start teaching this material to others within 24-48 hours of learning it yourself.

You will learn the foundational principles of leadership (influence) which will help you understand the importance of the following five questions. You will be able to take effective action by growing yourself and possibly others to a higher level of leadership (influence). Everything you ever achieve, internally and externally, will be a direct result of your influence.

1. ***Why* do we influence?** – Our character determines *why* we influence. Who we are on the inside is what matters. Do we manipulate or motivate? It's all about our intent.

2. ***How* do we influence?** – Our character, combined with our competency, determines *how* we influence. Who we are and what we know combine to create our unique style of influence which determines our methods of influence.

3. ***Where* do we influence?** – Our passion and purpose determine *where* we have the greatest influence. What motivates and inspires us gives us the energy and authenticity to motivate and inspire others.

4. ***Who* do we influence?** – We influence those *who* buy-in to us. Only those valuing and seeking what we value and seek will volunteer to follow us. They give us or deny us permission to influence them based on how well we have developed our character and competency.

5. ***When* do we influence?** – We influence others *when* they want our influence. We choose when

others influence us. Everyone else has the same choice. They decide when to accept or reject our influence.

The first three questions are about the choices we make as we lead (influence) ourselves and others. The last two questions deal more with the choices others will make as they decide first, *if* they will follow us, and second, *when* they will follow us. They will base their choices on *who we are* and *what we know*.

Asking these questions is important. Knowing the answers is more important. But, taking action based on the answers is most important. Cumulatively, the answers to these questions determine our leadership style and our level of influence (leadership).

On a scale of 1-10, your influence can be very low level (1) to very high level (10). But make no mistake, you *are* a leader. You *are* always on the scale. There is a positive and negative scale too. The higher on the scale you are the more effective you are. You will be at different levels with different people at different times depending on many different variables.

Someone thinking they are not a leader or someone that doesn't want to be a leader is still a leader. They will simply remain a low impact leader with low level influence getting low level results. They will likely spend much time frustrated with many areas of their life. Although they could influence a change, they choose instead to be primarily influenced by others.

What separates high impact leaders from low impact leaders? There are many things, but two primary differences are:

1) High impact leaders accept more responsibility in all areas of their lives while low impact leaders tend

to blame others and transfer responsibility more often.

2) High impact leaders have more positive influence while low impact leaders tend to have more negative influence.

My passion has led me to grow into my purpose which is to help others increase their influence personally and professionally while setting and reaching their goals. I am very passionate and have great conviction. I have realized many benefits by getting better results in all areas of my life. I have improved relationships with my family members, my friends, my associates, my peers, and my clients. I have witnessed people within these same groups embrace leadership principles and reap the same benefits.

The degree to which I *live* what I teach determines my effectiveness. My goal is to learn it, live it, and *then* teach it. I had major internal struggles as I grew my way to where I am. I'm a long way from perfect, so I seek daily improvement. Too often, I see people teaching leadership but not living what they're teaching. If I teach it, I live it.

My goal is to be a better leader tomorrow than I am today. I simply must get out of my own way and lead. I must lead me effectively before I can lead others effectively, not only with acquired knowledge, but also with experience from applying and living the principles.

I'll be transparent with personal stories to help you see how I have applied leadership principles by sharing: How I've struggled. How I've learned. How I've sacrificed. And, how I've succeeded.

Go beyond highlighting or underlining key points. Take the time to write down your thoughts related to the principle. Write down what you want to change. Write down how you can apply the principle in your life. You may want to consider getting a journal to fully capture your thoughts as you progress through the chapters. What you are thinking as you read is often much more important than what you're reading.

Most importantly, do not focus your thoughts on others. Yes, they need it too. We all need it. I need it. You need it. However, if you focus outside of yourself, you are missing the very point. Your influence comes from within. Your influence rises and falls based on your choices. You have untapped and unlimited potential waiting to be released. Only you can release it.

You, like everyone else, were born a leader. Now, let's take a leadership journey together.

(If you enjoyed this Introduction to *Defining Influence*, it is available in paperback, audio, and as an eBook on Amazon.com)

Excerpt from

10 Values of High Impact Leaders

Our values are the foundation upon which we build our character. I'll be sharing 10 values high impact leaders work to master because they know these values will have a tremendous impact on their ability to lead others well. You may be thinking, *"Aren't there more than 10 leadership values?"* Absolutely! They seem to be endless. And, they are all important. These are simply 10 key values which I have chosen to highlight.

Since leadership is very dynamic and complex, the more values you have been able to internalize and utilize synergistically together, the more effective you will be. The more influence you will have.

"High performing organizations that continuously invest in leadership development are now defining new 21st century leadership models to deal with today's gaps in their leadership pipelines and the new global business environment. These people-focused organizations have generated nearly 60% improved business growth, reported a 66% improvement in bench strength, and showed a 62% improvement in employee retention. And, our research shows that it is not enough to just spend money on leadership training, but rather to follow specific practices that drive accelerated business results." ~ Josh Bersin

Do you want to become a high impact leader?

I believe everyone is a leader, but they are leading at different levels.

I believe everyone can and should lead from *where they are.*

I believe everyone can and should make a high impact.

I believe growth doesn't just happen; we must make it happen.

I believe before you will invest in yourself you must first believe in yourself.

I believe leaders must believe in their team before they will invest in their team.

I truly believe *everything rises and falls on influence.*

There is a story of a tourist who paused for a rest in a small town in the mountains. He went over to an old man sitting on a bench in front of the only store in town and inquired, *"Friend, can you tell me something this town is noted for?"*

"Well," replied the old man, *"I don't rightly know except it's the starting point to the world. You can start here and go anywhere you want."* [1]

That's a great little story. We are all at *"the starting point"* to the world, and we *"can start here and go anywhere we want."* We can expand our influence 360° in all directions by starting in the center with ourselves.

Consider the following illustration. Imagine you are standing in the center. You can make a high impact. However, it will not happen by accident. You must become intentional. You must live with purpose while focusing on your performance as you develop your potential.

Note: Illustration and 10 Values are listed on the following pages.

Why we do what we do is about our *purpose*.

How we do what we do is about our *performance*.

What we do will determine our *potential*.

Where these three components overlap, you will achieve a **HIGH IMPACT**.

10 Values of High Impact Leaders

1
THE VALUE OF VISION
Vision is the foundation of hope.
"When there's hope in the future, there's power in the present." ~ Les Brown

2
THE VALUE OF MODELING
Someone is always watching you.
"Who we are on the inside is what people see on the outside." ~ Mack Story

3
THE VALUE OF RESPONSIBILITY
When we take responsibility,
we take control.
"What is common sense is not always common practice." ~ Stephen R. Covey

4
THE VALUE OF TIMING
It matters when you do what you do.
"It's about doing the right thing for the right reason at the right time." ~ Mack Story

5
THE VALUE OF RESPECT
To be respected, we must be respectful.
"Go See, ask why, and show respect"
~ Jim Womack

6
THE VALUE OF EMPOWERMENT
Leaders gain influence by
giving it to others.
"Leadership is not reserved for leaders."
~ Marcus Buckingham

7
THE VALUE OF DELEGATION
We should lead with questions
instead of directions.
"Delegation 101: Delegating 'what to do,' makes you responsible. Delegating 'what to accomplish,' allows others to become responsible."
~ Mack Story

8
THE VALUE OF MULTIPLICATION
None of us is as influential as all of us.
"To add growth, lead followers. To multiply, lead leaders." ~ John C. Maxwell

9
THE VALUE OF RESULTS
Leaders like to make things happen.
"Most people fail in the getting started."
~ Maureen Falcone

10
THE VALUE OF SIGNIFICANCE
Are you going to settle for success?
"Significance is a choice that only successful people can make."
~ Mack Story

Excerpt (Chapter 3 of 30) from
Blue-Collar Leadership® & Culture:
The 5 Components for Building High Performance Teams

THE IMPACT OF CULTURE

THOSE WHO WORK THERE WILL DETERMINE WHO WANTS TO WORK THERE

"I think the most important and difficult thing is to create a culture in the organization where leadership is really important. It's important for people in the company to realize that this is a growth-oriented company, and the biggest thing we have to grow here is you, because it's you who will make this company better by your own growth. ~ Jim Blanchard

Listen to the voices of leaders who are losing the labor war:

- "We just can't find any good people."
  As if…there aren't any good or great people.
- "Due to the low unemployment rate, there just aren't any good people left."
  As if…the only people who can be offered a job are those without a job.
- "In today's labor market, those who want to work are already working."
  As if…those who are working at one place can't decide to work at a different place.
- "When we do get good people, they won't stay."
  As if…the problem is always with the people and never with their leaders.

One thing I know about leaders who make these and

similar comments is this: Their culture is a competitive disadvantage. Someone else has the advantage and is winning the battle for the good and great people. The good and great people certainly aren't out of work wishing they had a job. They're working someplace else.

Until a leader is aware of the problem, they can't address the problem. In case it's not obvious, the problem is their culture. The leader owns this problem whether they want to or not. Every time I hear these comments, and I hear them a lot, I know I'm talking to a leader who doesn't know what they don't know.

Ria and I hear leaders across varying blue-collar and white-collar industries repeatedly making these comments as we travel across the USA speaking on leadership development. These voices seem to be getting louder and louder. In fact, these voices are an inspiration for this book.

There are many leaders in blue-collar industries needing help. I want to help them stop searching for good people and start attracting great people. The transformation won't happen overnight. However, until it starts happening, it's not going to happen. My intention is to use this book to raise awareness while providing a transformational road map for those leaders who want to make their culture their greatest competitive advantage.

We were speaking in Louisville, KY recently to owners of blue-collar organizations. Afterward, one approached and said, "There isn't a magic pill is there? I think we all hoped there was." I replied, "No sir. There isn't a magic pill or an easy button. This is how you build a high performance team and an exceptional culture that will attract, retain, and support them. There is no other way."

Your culture is always attracting certain types of people and repelling others. Who we are is who we attract. This principle applies to individuals as well as organizations. The culture within your organization is negatively or positively impacting those within the organization, and some who are outside the organization.

The key point is to understand the people inside your organization are constantly providing the most influential type of advertising about your organization and the leaders within it. It's called word of mouth advertising. How your team is feeling inside the organization will determine what they're saying outside the organization.

If what they're saying about their leaders and the organization to others is good, it'll be easier to find good people. If what they're saying is great, it'll be easier to attract great people. But, if what they're saying is bad, finding good people will be hard, if not impossible.

Remember the voices at the start of this chapter? Those leaders had team members who were sharing bad word of mouth advertising about the organization. Unless those leaders choose to change, nothing will change.

Common sense reveals it's easier to win the labor war while attracting great people instead of searching for good people. However, what's common sense isn't always common practice. Often, it takes uncommon sense to act on things that are commonly understood. Creating an organizational culture that will attract and retain great people requires leaders with uncommon sense.

The best led companies aren't impacted by labor shortages because they're consistently attracting the best and the brightest people to their organizations.

"If we lose sight of people, we lose sight of the very purpose of leadership." ~ Tony Dungy

Excerpt (Trait 4 of 30) from
Blue-Collar Leadership® & Teamwork:
30 Traits of High Impact Players

BE RESPONSIBLE

MAKING THIS CHOICE GIVES YOU A VOICE

"Total responsibility for failure is a difficult thing to accept, and taking ownership when things go wrong requires extraordinary humility and courage."
~ Jocko Willink

The higher we climb up the organizational chart or the higher we climb up the pay scale, the harder it is for many of us to remain humble. However, as high impact team players, it's our responsibility to choose to be humble regardless of our status or income. And if necessary, it's also our responsibility to learn what it truly means to be humble.

Humility is a choice that high impact players will make.

If you haven't accomplished much or done much, it's a little easier to remain humble. I believe as a whole the blue-collar workforce is naturally more humble simply because of who we are and where we come from. However, I also believe some who climb their way up from the entry-level positions let it go to their heads.

I want to remain a humble high impact player. That's on me. Not letting my success go to my head is my responsibility. I've also gone a step farther and made helping others do the same my responsibility. High impact team players always do more than is required.

Each of us is responsible for choosing our values and

those values will determine our circumstances and the impact we have, especially when it comes to teamwork.

Just as humility is sometimes a hard choice for those with a high position or status, taking responsibility is often a hard choice for those in a low position or status. But as I've learned over the years, taking responsibility seems to be a hard choice for many regardless of their title, position, rank, status, or income.

When it comes to teamwork, low impact players dodge responsibility like it's a deadly disease. They may disappear when the task is being addressed or begin to make excuses as to why they can't help and shouldn't be asked to help. That creates distrust.

High impact players know a secret: When low impact players are whining, it's easy to start shining. They also know how to shine. It's actually pretty simple. They just listen for whining, and then step up and say, "I'll do it."

At that moment, the high impact player builds trust by simply taking the responsibility. The next responsibility of the high impact player is to follow through and get results. If they don't, they will create distrust with the team and the leaders. If they do, they will build additional trust with the team and the leaders.

Leaders are ultimately responsible for making things happen. If they don't make things happen, it won't be long before they are replaced by someone else who will be given the same mission. High impact players know the quickest way to build trust with a leader is to help them get results, so that's what they focus on doing.

As they develop a reputation for helping the leaders get results, their influence increases with those leaders. Because of their choice (taking responsibility and following through), they earn a voice. As time passes, the high impact players are asked their opinions much more often than the low impact players.

As a result, the high impact players begin to influence the leader's choices and the team's direction. They're still on the team, but they're playing at much higher level. Those who are willing to make things happen are also given more chances to make things happen.

High impact players are never just along for the ride. They want to drive. They see the big picture. They don't shy away from responsibility. They wake up everyday looking for an opportunity to shine.

Imagine a team full of low impact players where everyone is dodging responsibility on every front. The leader will be frustrated, and the team will be frustrated. And little, if anything, will get accomplished. Unfortunately, these types of teams are common. Depending on your circumstances, it may be too easy to imagine this team. If so, don't miss what's right in front of you: endless opportunities to shine.

Now imagine a very different team, one filled with high impact players. They could be given the exact same mission as the frustrated low impact team. However, no one would be frustrated. The mission would be accomplished. Instead of being focused on finding excuses, the entire team would be focused on finding a way to make it happen. In that case, everyone shines.

What's the major difference between the two teams above? Attitude. Low impact players tend to have a negative attitude. High impact players always have a positive attitude. Attitude is a choice. If we can choose to be positive or negative, why not choose to be positive.

"Responsibility includes two important ideas – choosing right over wrong and accepting ownership for one's conduct and obligations." ~ Charles G. Koch

Excerpt (Ch. 5 of 30) from
Blue-Collar Leadership®:
Leading from the Front Lines

THERE IS AN "I" IN TEAM

EVERY TEAM IS MADE OF "I"NDIVIDUALS

"I'm just a plowhand from Arkansas, but I have learned how to hold a team together – how to lift some men up, how to calm others down, until finally they've got one heartbeat together as a team. There's always just three things I say: 'If anything goes bad, I did it. If anything goes semi-good, then we did it. If anything goes real good, they did it.' That's all it takes to get people to win." ~ Paul "Bear" Bryant

Paul *"Bear"* Bryant was one of the greatest college football coaches to ever lead a team of young men down the field. He was also a *"plowhand"* from Arkansas. A blue-collar worker. The blue-collar world has produced some of the greatest leaders of all time, so you should be proud and hold your head high. *Without them, the world as we know it would not exist.*

There's nothing holding you back but you. As my blue-collar friend, Donovan Weldon, stated so well, *"The only person between you and success is you. MOVE! The only person between you and failure is you. STAND FIRM!"* Those are strong words of wisdom. Donovan started on the bottom just like you and me. But today, he's the CEO of Donovan Industrial Service in Orange, TX near Beaumont.

Donovan's success didn't happen by accident. He made it happen. You can make things happen too! He's a blue-collar leader that believes in and develops his team on a regular basis. I know because my wife, Ria, and I had the privilege of being brought in to speak to his team about leadership in 2014. They are making it happen on purpose for a purpose!

It's time for you to stop playing small and start playing tall.

A college degree is not required for you to play at a higher level. Not having one is simply an excuse some people use to continue playing small. If you want a college degree, use what you will learn on these pages to find a way to get one. If you don't want a college degree, use what you learn on these pages to make it happen without one.

You are the key to your success. You must believe in yourself. You must grow and develop yourself, which is what you're doing as you read this book. Do not stop growing! And when the time is right, you must bet on yourself.

Understanding your role as a team member is another must. Those on the front lines often underestimate themselves because they can't see the big picture. They can't see the value they have to offer. Far too often, their boss isn't a high impact leader and needs a lot of growth and development too. Bosses are often given the title without any formal development.

When I write about the front lines on these pages, I'm not only talking about the people in entry level positions. They are obviously on the front lines, but they also have leaders that are on the front lines with them and various team members supporting them too. They can all learn from these pages.

This book was written specifically for anyone at any level that visits, interacts with, or works on the front lines.

The principles I share with you must be applied if you want to make a high impact and be recognized for leading from the front lines. Regardless of your position, the more you apply these principles, the more options you will have, and the more positions you will be offered as you climb even higher.

Teams are made up of "I"ndividuals, so there are many I's on every team, regardless of how many times you hear, *"There is no 'I' in TEAM."* As a matter of fact, *you are one of them.* Every person on a team is an "I" and has the potential to lead (influence) the team, positively or negatively.

"Leadership is influence. Nothing more. Nothing less."
~ John C. Maxwell

You must understand there are many official and unofficial teams in the organization where you work. They are very dynamic and constantly changing.

When most of us think of which team we are on, we immediately think of our peers, the ones on the same crew, in the same department, or working on the same job. This is our core team, but it only represents the smallest team we're on. We also support other teams too, as others support our team.

When we choose to contribute beyond our immediate team, we are choosing to be part of a bigger team. Often, this only requires a choice to do so. Your choice to get involved in other areas sends a clear message to the high impact leaders.

When you play tall, you choose to contribute because you know it will increase your influence and your impact on the front lines. If you want to play tall, you should want to be noticed, to be selected, to volunteer, to share information, to accept more responsibility, and ultimately, to make a contribution at a higher level.

As a direct result of your choice to step up, your influence increases. You're demonstrating you can lead from the front lines and will be seen and respected by all high impact leaders as a high impact leader. Your actions will not go unnoticed.

When you play small, you choose not to contribute because you don't want to do more. If your goal is to coast until pay day, it won't be a secret you can keep. When you make every effort not to be noticed, not to be selected, not to volunteer, not to share information, not to accept responsibility, and ultimately to not contribute, *you will absolutely be noticed*.

As a direct result of your choice not to step up, your influence decreases. Your influence on the front lines and with your leaders will be diminished. You are more likely to become reactive and frustrated blaming others for what you have chosen. Blaming others will further reduce your influence.

You first make your choices, then your choices make you.

"The most valuable player is the one that makes the most players valuable." ~ Peyton Manning

Excerpt (Ch. 4 of 30) from
Blue-Collar Leadership® & Supervision:
Unleash Your Team's Potential

UNDERSTANDING ARTIFICIAL INFLUENCE

THERE IS A DIFFERENCE BETWEEN SOMEONE RESPECTING YOUR POSITION AND SOMEONE RESPECTING YOU

"Into the hands of every individual is given a marvelous power for good or evil - the silent, unconscious, unseen influence of his life. This is simply the constant radiation of what man really is, not what he pretends to be."
~ William George Jordan

If you want to begin to lead beyond your position, you must be respected by those you want to influence. No one gives you respect. You can demand respect all day long, but it's a waste of time. I always laugh (on the inside) when I hear someone demand respect. You will never be respected because you demand to be respected, at work or at home. It's simply not going to happen.

Think about it from your own point of view. If there's a boss or manager you don't like because of who they are as a person, can they demand respect from you and get it? Absolutely not. You may respect their position. But, you will never respect them simply because they demand it. You *must* respect their position to *keep* your job. But, you don't have to respect *them* to keep your job.

A position will give you authority but not influence. Influence must be earned by first earning respect. The more you are respected the more influence you will gain. Everything I'm sharing in this book, *if applied*, will help you earn respect and increase your influence with others.

Having a position or title such as Mom, Dad, Coach, Boss, Supervisor, Manager, VP, President, CEO, Owner, etc. gives you authority and control over other people. I call this *artificial influence*. Artificial influence creates the *illusion* that you have *real* influence. However, if you choose to influence people using only artificial influence, you are not leading. You are simply managing. Sure you may accomplish a lot, but what are you leaving on the table?

You can easily validate the principle of artificial influence by considering those bosses you've had, or now have, that you would never follow if they didn't control your pay, your time off, your promotions, etc. If you only follow a boss because you *have to*, their influence is *not* real. It's artificial. And unfortunately for the company, most likely, you will only do what you have to do.

The title of boss is one that is simply given, often by another manager with artificial influence. However, when it comes to real influence, managers are not in the same league as leaders. If you develop real influence based on character-based principles that you have internalized, then you will *earn* the right to lead. When you do, those reporting to you will do much *more than they have to* simply because they *respect* you.

A high impact leader operates from a position of real influence, not artificial influence or authority.

Listen to the voices of those with *artificial* influence:
- How am I supposed to make something happen when those people don't report to me?
- I can't make them do anything. They don't report to me and won't do anything I tell them to do.
- I can't get anything done in that department. They report to someone else, not me. It's useless to try.
- How can I be responsible for their results when they don't report to me?
- If you want me to make it happen, you've got to give me authority over those people.
- My hands are tied. They don't report to me.

Phrases like those are always spoken by a manager, never by

a leader. I've heard them spoken many times in my career by managers who don't have a clue about leadership. The only influence they have at work is directly tied to the *authority, artificial influence*, which is associated with the position they hold. Without it, they wouldn't accomplish much of anything.

I remember being in a facility as a consultant once. I needed some help from a few team members in a different department, so I asked the manager I was working with if it would be okay if I went over and asked them for some help. He said, *"You'll have to wait. I'll have to get an interpreter because none of them speak English."* I said, *"Okay, I'll go wait over there."* I thought it was interesting. When I got there, they all spoke English to me. Leadership is influence.

Managers make things happen with people who *have to* help them. Leaders make things happen with people who *want to* help them.

Most managers have never read a leadership book and can't understand a leader doesn't need authority to make something happen. Leaders only need *influence* to make something happen. Leadership is *not* about who *has* to help you. Leadership *is* about who *wants* to help you.

Research studies have repeatedly shown a 40% productivity increase when comparing people who *want to* follow a leader with those who *have to* follow a manager.

A manager thrives on artificial influence and is not interested in developing himself or others in order to capture this massive loss of productivity. That's what leaders do, not managers.

How do you influence? What is your style? Are you a director or a connector? Do you tell or sell? What would change if you had more real influence in every situation?

"When we look at people who disobey their leaders, the first question we ought to ask is not, 'What's wrong with those people?' but rather, 'What's wrong with their leader?' It says that responsibility begins at the top."
~ Malcolm Gladwell

Excerpt (Ch. 26 of 30) from
Blue-Collar Kaizen:
Leading Lean & Lean Teams

LEVERAGE THE TEAM

FOCUS ON STRENGTHS; DEVELOP WEAKNESSES

"Instead of focusing on weaknesses, give your attention to people's strengths. Focus on sharpening skills that already exist. Compliment positive qualities. Bring out the gifts inherent in them. Weaknesses can wait unless they are character flaws. Only after you have developed a strong rapport with the person and they have begun to grow and gain confidence should you address areas of weakness...and then those should be handled gently and one at a time."
~ John C. Maxwell

High impact Lean leaders have a gift for turning a group of people into a team in a short period of time.

At the start of a kaizen event, calling the group of people a team is a poor use of the word team. They are simply a group of people assembled in a room about to be given a task to accomplish together. Most often, some want to be there, and some don't want to be there. Odds are, this specific group of people has never worked together on a project before.

Knowing about continuous improvement is a must if you're going to lead a kaizen event. However, knowing about continuous improvement (your competency) will not be the key to turning a group of people into a team of people. Turning a group of people into a team of people is about having respect for the people. Your ability to quickly build a strong, functional team will be determined primarily by your character and secondarily by your competency. Your character is key in this area.

I've seen some very talented Lean leaders and others who have an extensive in-depth knowledge of Lean attempt to lead kaizen events. Most often, they struggle from the moment the event kicks off until the end. They know a lot about Lean but very little about leading people effectively. Why? Because their focus has been on learning Lean, not on learning leadership.

When it comes to growing, developing, and creating a new team, high impact Lean leaders know to focus on the team member's strengths in their area of competency and to develop their weaknesses in the area of character.

Each team member's competency strengths (what they know and can do), if leveraged, will launch the team forward. Each team member's character weaknesses (who they are) will hold the team back. This includes you.

High impact Lean leaders know there are always character issues. We all have them. A few of us are constantly working to improving ourselves, but many of us aren't. Focusing on character weaknesses is why high impact Lean leaders blend leadership development and personal growth components into all of their continuous improvement initiatives.

This is why I utilize the 20/80 rule I taught you in chapter 19. I didn't start using it by accident. I started using it by design. Until then, I only focused on leveraging the team's strengths. But, I hadn't been focused on developing their weaknesses. I'm sure you already know the root cause of most major problems that arise during kaizen events, whether with team members or people not on the team, is rooted in character issues.

The majority of Lean leaders focus only on the continuous improvement (competency) component of Lean. As a result, they provide no leadership in the area that will hold them and the team back the most, character development.

The reason Lean leaders do not address character development during kaizen events is because many of them are not addressing it in their own lives. In other words, because they are not leading themselves well, they cannot lead others well. Character development is always the missing link personally and professionally.

In the area of competency, ask questions and generate discussions to find out what people like or don't like to do. Don't assume they like to do what they are paid to do. I always have everyone introduce and speak about themselves before I talk about anything. I ask what their job is, how long they have been with the organization, what their previous job was, what their hobbies are, what they do for fun, how much Lean and event experience they have, and I ask them to tell me about their family.

The answers to these questions and the associated discussions allow me to connect and learn about their strengths. Then, I'm positioned to leverage the team.

"Humility means knowing and using your strength for the benefit of others, on behalf of a higher purpose. The humble leader is not weak, but strong...is not preoccupied with self, but with how best to use his or her strengths for the good of others. A humble leader does not think less of himself, but chooses to consider the needs of others in fulfilling a worthy cause. We love to be in the presence of a humble leader because they bring out the very best in us. Their focus is on our purpose, our contribution, and our ability to accomplish all we set out to accomplish." ~ Alan Ross

Order books online at Amazon or TopStoryLeadership.com

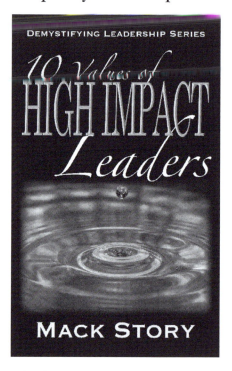

High impact leaders align their habits with key values in order to maximize their influence. High impact leaders intentionally grow and develop themselves in an effort to more effectively grow and develop others.

These *10 Values* are commonly understood. However, they are not always commonly practiced. These *10 Values* will help you build trust and accelerate relationship building. Those mastering these *10 Values* will be able to lead with speed as they develop 360° of influence from wherever they are.

Order books online at Amazon or TopStoryLeadership.com

Are you looking for transformation in your life? Do you want better results? Do you want stronger relationships?

In *Defining Influence*, Mack breaks down many of the principles that will allow anyone at any level to methodically and intentionally increase their positive influence.

Mack blends his personal growth journey with lessons on the principles he learned along the way. He's not telling you what he learned after years of research, but rather what he learned from years of application and transformation. Everything rises and falls on influence.

Order books online at Amazon or TopStoryLeadership.com

10 Foundational Elements of Intentional Transformation serves as a source of motivation and inspiration to help you climb your way to the next level and beyond as you learn to intentionally create a better future for yourself. The pages will ENCOURAGE, ENGAGE, and EMPOWER you as you become more focused and intentional about moving from where you are to where you want to be.

All of us are somewhere, but most of us want to be somewhere else. However, we don't always know how to get there. You will learn how to intentionally move forward as you learn to navigate the 10 foundational layers of transformation.

Order books online at Amazon or TopStoryLeadership.com

"Sales persuasion and influence, moving others, has changed more in the last 10 years than it has in the last 100 years. It has transitioned from buyer beware to seller beware" ~ *Daniel Pink*

So, it's no longer *"Buyer beware!"* It's *"Seller beware!"* Why? Today, the buyer has the advantage over the seller. Most often, they are holding it in their hand. It's a smart phone. They can learn everything about your product before they meet you. They can compare features and prices instantly. The major advantage you do still have is: YOU! IF they like you. IF they trust you. IF they feel you want to help them.

This book is filled with 30 short chapters providing unique insights that will give you the advantage, not over the buyer, but over your competition: those who are selling what you're selling. It will help you sell yourself.

Order books online at Amazon or BlueCollarLeadership.com

It's easier to compete when you're attracting great people instead of searching for good people.

Blue-Collar Leadership® & Culture will help you understand why culture is the key to becoming a sought after employer of choice within your industry and in your area of operation.

You'll also discover how to leverage the components of The Transformation Equation to create a culture that will support, attract, and retain high performance team members.

Blue-Collar Leadership® & Culture is intended to serve as a tool, a guide, and a transformational road map for leaders who want to create a high impact culture that will become their greatest competitive advantage.

Order books online at Amazon or BlueCollarLeadership.com

(Also available in Spanish)

Are you ready to play at the next level and beyond?

In today's high stakes game of business, the players on the team are the competitive advantage for any organization. But, only if they are on the field instead of on the bench.

The competitive advantage for every individual is developing 360° of influence regardless of position, title, or rank.

Blue-Collar Leadership® & Teamwork provides a simple, yet powerful and unique, resource for individuals who want to increase their influence and make a high impact. It's also a resource and tool for leaders, teams, and organizations, who are ready to Engage the Front Line to Improve the Bottom Line.

Order books online at Amazon or BlueCollarLeadership.com

"I wish someone would have given me these books 30 years ago when I started my career on the front lines. They would have launched my career then. They can launch your career now." ~ Mack Story

Blue-Collar Leadership® and *Blue-Collar Leadership® & Supervision* were written specifically for those working on the front lines and those who are leading them. With 30 short, easy to read 3 page chapters, these books contain powerful, yet simple to understand leadership principles and lessons.

Note: These two Blue-Collar Leadership® books are the blue-collar version of the MAXIMIZE books and contain nearly identical content.

Download the first 5 chapters of these books FREE at: BlueCollarLeadership.com/download

Order books online at Amazon or BlueCollarLeadership.com

The biggest challenge in process improvement and cultural transformation isn't identifying the problems. It's execution: implementing and sustaining the solutions.

Blue-Collar Kaizen is a resource for anyone in any position who is, or will be, leading a team through process improvement and change. Learn to engage, empower, and encourage your team for long term buy-in and sustained gains.

Mack Story has over 11,000 hours experience leading hundreds of leaders and thousands of their cross-functional kaizen team members through process improvement, organizational change, and cultural transformation. He shares lessons learned from his experience and many years of studying, teaching, and applying leadership principles.

Order books online at Amazon or TopStoryLeadership.com

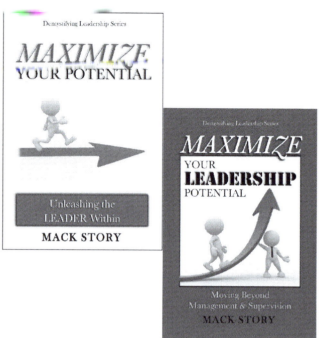

"I wish someone had given me these books 30 years ago when I started my career. They would have changed my life then. They can change your life now." ~ Mack Story

MAXIMIZE Your Potential will help you learn to lead yourself well. *MAXIMIZE Your Leadership Potential* will help you learn to lead others well. With 30 short, easy to read 3 page chapters, these books contain simple and easy to understand, yet powerful leadership lessons.

Note: These two MAXIMIZE books are the white-collar, or non-specific, version of the Blue-Collar Leadership® books and contain nearly identical content.

ABOUT RIA STORY

Mack's wife, Ria, is also a motivational leadership speaker, author, and a world class coach who has a unique ability to help people develop and achieve their life and career goals and guide them in building the habits and discipline to achieve their personal view of greatness. Ria brings a wealth of personal experience in working with clients to achieve their personal goals and aspirations in a way few coaches can.

Like many, Ria has faced adversity in life. Raised on an isolated farm in Alabama, she suffered extreme sexual abuse by her father from age 12 to 19. Desperate to escape, she left home at 19 without a job, a car, or even a high school diploma. Ria learned to be resilient, and not just survive, but thrive. (Watch her 7 minute TEDx talk at RiaStory.com/TEDx) She worked her way through school, acquiring an MBA with a 4.0 GPA, and eventually resigned from her career in the corporate world to pursue a passion for helping others achieve success.

Ria's background includes more than 10 years in healthcare administration, including several years in management, and later, Director of Compliance and Regulatory Affairs for a large healthcare organization. Ria's responsibilities included oversight of thousands of organizational policies, organizational compliance with all State and Federal regulations, and responsibility for several million dollars in Medicare appeals.

Ria co-founded Top Story Leadership, which offers leadership speaking, training, coaching, and consulting.

Ria's Story From Ashes To Beauty
by Ria Story

The unforgettable story and inspirational memoir of a young woman who was extremely sexually abused by her father from age 12 to 19 and then rejected by her mother. (Watch 7 minutes of her story in her TEDx talk at RiaStory.com/TEDx)

For the first time, Ria publicly reveals details of the extreme sexual abuse she endured growing up. 13 years after leaving home at 19, she decided to speak out about her story and encourage others to find hope and healing.

Determined to not only survive, but also thrive, Ria shares how she was able to overcome the odds and find hope and healing to Achieve Abundant Life. She shares the leadership principles she applied to find professional success, personal significance, and details how she was able to find the courage to share her story to give hope to others around the world.

Ria states, *"It would be easier for me to let this story go untold forever and simply move on with life…One of the most difficult things I've ever done is write this book. Victims of sexual assault or abuse don't want to talk because they want to avoid the social stigma and the fear of not being believed or the possibility of being blamed for something that was not their fault. My hope and prayer is someone will benefit from learning how I was able to overcome such difficult circumstances. That brings purpose to the pain and reason enough to share what I would rather have left behind forever. Our scars make us stronger."*

Available at Amazon.com in paperback, audio, and eBook. To order your signed copy, to learn more about Ria, or to book her to speak at your event, please visit: **RiaStory.com/TEDx**

Order books online at Amazon or RiaStory.com

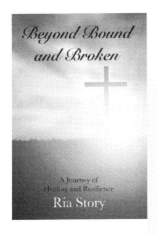

Ria Story

In *Beyond Bound and Broken,* Ria shares how she overcame the shame, fear, and doubt she developed after enduring years of extreme sexual abuse by her father. Forced to play the role of a wife and even shared with other men due to her father's perversions, Ria left home at 19 without a job, a car, or even a high-school diploma. This book also contains lessons on resilience and overcoming adversity that you can apply to your own life.

In *Ria's Story From Ashes To Beauty*, Ria tells her personal story of growing up as a victim of extreme sexual abuse from age 12 – 19, leaving home to escape, and her decision to tell her story. She shares her heart in an attempt to help others overcome their own adversity.

Order books online at Amazon or RiaStory.com

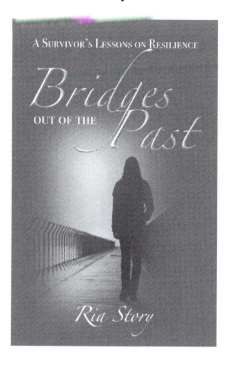

It's not what happens to you in life. It's who you become because of it. We all experience pain, grief, and loss in life. Resilience is the difference between *"I didn't die,"* and *"I learned to live again."* In this captivating book on resilience, Ria walks you through her own horrific story of more than seven years of sexual abuse by her father. She then shares how she learned not only to survive, but also to thrive in spite of her past. Learn how to overcome challenges, obstacles, and adversity in your own life by building a bridge out of the past and into the future.

(Watch 7 minutes of her story at RiaStory.com/TEDx)

Order books online at Amazon or RiaStory.com

You have untapped potential to do, have, and be more in life. But, developing your potential and becoming the best version of yourself will require personal transformation. You will have to transform from who you are today into who you want to become tomorrow.

Gain unique insight in, *"Fearfully and Wonderfully Me: Become the Woman You are Destined to Be"* and the accompanying workbook to help you: believe in yourself and your potential; embrace your self-worth; overcome self-limiting beliefs; increase your influence personally & professionally; and achieve your goals & develop a mindset for success. These two resources will empower you to own your story, write a new chapter, and become the woman and leader you are destined to be.

Order books online at Amazon or RiaStory.com

You have untapped potential waiting to be unlocked. To be successful requires us to have knowledge of the principles of success, awareness of how to utilize them, and discipline to intentionally apply them. There are no shortcuts to success, but we can travel much faster when we have an achievement model we can apply. This model will help you develop more influence personally and professionally, execute an action plan for personal success, and maximize your potential in life. Both women and men alike will find practical and relevant information to immediately apply to their situation and improve the outcome.

Order books online at Amazon or RiaStory.com

Note: Leadership Gems is the generic, non-gender specific, version of Leadership Gems for Women. The content is very similar.

Women are naturally high level leaders because they are relationship oriented. However, it's a *"man's world"* out there and natural ability isn't enough to help you be successful as a leader. You must be intentional.

Ria packed these books with 30 leadership gems which very successful people internalize and apply. Ria has combined her years of experience in leadership roles of different organizations along with years of studying, teaching, training, and speaking on leadership to give you these 30, short and simple, yet powerful and profound, lessons to help you become very successful, regardless of whether you are in a formal leadership position or not.

Order books online at Amazon or RiaStory.com

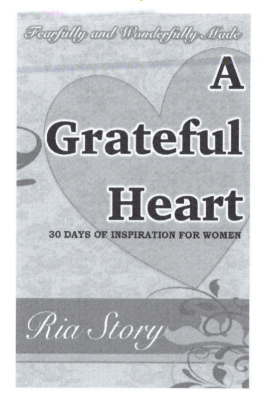

Become inspired by this 30-day collection of daily devotions for women, where you will find practical advice on intentionally living with a grateful heart, inspirational quotes, short journaling opportunities, and scripture from God's Word on practicing gratitude.

Motivational Planning Journals
Choose a theme for the season of your life!
Now available at Amazon.com or RiaStory.com

Start each day with a purposeful mindset, and you will achieve your priorities based on your values.

Just a few minutes of intentional thought every morning will allow you to focus your energy, increase your influence, and make your day all that it can be!

Each journal in the series has different motivational quotes and a motivational theme. Choose one or get all six for an entire year's worth of **Motivational Planning**!

Order books online at Amazon or RiaStory.com

Ria's *Effective Leadership Series* books are written to develop and enhance your leadership skills, while also helping you increase your abilities in areas like communication and relationships, time management, planning and execution, leading and implementing change. Look for more books in the *Effective Leadership Series*:

- *Straight Talk: The Power of Effective Communication*

- *PRIME Time: The Power of Effective Planning*

- *Change Happens: Leading Yourself and Others through Change (Co-authored by Ria & Mack Story)*

Top Story Leadership

Leadership Speaking & Development
Leadership Made Simple

- Leadership Development/Personal Growth
- Cultural Change/Transformation
- Communication/Trust/Relationships
- Time Management/Planning/Execution

Top Story Leadership simplifies foundational leadership principles into everyday language and easy to apply and understand concepts, so organizations and individuals can turn potential into reality. Mack and Ria Story are Certified Speakers and Trainers. They are published authors with more than 32 books available on leadership development, personal growth, and inspirational topics.

- Equip Organizational Leaders
- Encourage Positive Change
- Educate & Empower
- Engage the Front Line to Improve the Bottom Line

What clients have to say...

"My first words are, GET SIGNED UP! This training is not, and I stress, not your everyday leadership seminar! I have attended dozens and sent hundreds to the so-called 'Leadership-Training.' I can tell you that while all of the courses, classes, webinars, and seminars, had good intentions, nothing can touch what Mack and Ria Story provide. I just wish I had it 20 years ago!"
~ **Sam McLamb, VP & COO, CMP**

"We would highly recommend Mack and Ria as speakers...their presentation was inspirational, thought-provoking, and filled with humor. They taught us some foundational leadership principles."
~ **Stephen, President-elect, WCR**

"Mack and Ria understand people! The dynamic team made such an impact on our front line supervision that they were begging for more training! We highly recommend Mack and Ria!"
~ ***Rebecca, Director of Process Improvement, GKN***

LEADERSHIP Call Us Today!
334.332.3526
info@TopStoryLeadership.com
TopStoryLeadership.com

BlueCollarLeadership.com

Helping Leaders Engage the Front Line to Improve the Bottom Line

Are you ready to turn your greatest asset into your greatest advantage?

What clients have to say

"My first words are, GET SIGNED UP! This training is not, and I stress, no! your everyday leadership seminar! I have attended dozens and sent hundreds to the so-called 'Leadership Training.' I can tell you that while all of the courses, classes, webinars, and seminars, had good intentions, nothing can touch what Mack and Ria Story provide. I just wish I had it 20 years ago!"
~Sam McLamb, VP & COO, CMP

"Joining forces with Mack was a revolutionary opportunity for our company. We have achieved incredible results while witnessing the growth and development of our associates as they have been empowered."
~ Justin Saunders, CFO Madix, Inc

"Having worked in manufacturing plants for most of my 30 year career, I found Mack Story's Blue-Collar Leadership to be a very practical guide for all who aspire to lead, with or without a title."
~ Amir Ghannad, Campbell's Soup & Author of The Transformative Leader

Blue-Collar Leadership® provides leaders with a platform for training and developing their workforce to unleash their potential by taking powerful leadership concepts and packaging them in easy to understand and apply resources for:

- Transforming the Culture
- Equipping the Leaders
- Engaging the Front Line
- Encouraging Positive Change
- Empowering Lean/Kaizen Leaders

Mack Story, founder of Blue-Collar Leadership®, logged 11,000+ hours leading cross-functional teams and has 30+ years of experience in the blue-collar manufacturing industry. He is a certified leadership speaker, trainer, and author of 14 leadership books, including 10 Values of High Impact Leaders and Defining Influence, as well as the Blue-Collar Leadership® Series books.

334-728-4143
Mack@MackStory.com
BlueCollarLeadership.com

ENGAGE Your
FRONT LINE
To IMPROVE the
BOTTOM LINE!

If you're willing to invest in your Blue-Collar team, I am too!

~Mack Story

Limited Time Special Offer:

Take advantage of our "Special Offer Package" which includes: a greatly reduced speaking fee, hundreds of FREE books (choose from a mix of our 32 titles), up to 2 hours of on site speaking or training, plus we pay all of our expenses. For current details, visit:
BlueCollarLeadership.com/Special-Offer

*Restrictions apply.

"My first words are, GET SIGNED UP! This training is not, and I stress, not your everyday leadership seminar!" Sam, VP & COO

Made in the USA
Monee, IL
07 September 2024